I0459288

Get Up and Fight

By Poupy Gaelle Nguetsop

Dedication

I dedicate this book first, to my dad who passed away in 2023, who wasn't able to beat his liver cancer. Then to all aspiring journalists and women entrepreneurs who struggle in life finding their pathways to succeed and finally, to all those victims of domestic violence and sexual abuse all over the world **especially in Africa.**

Table of Contents

Chapter 1: A Retro From My Childhood To Now

From a very young age, I developed an entrepreneurial spirit, just like my dad. I have always wished to work for myself, to put my skills and ideas out into the world for people to see and benefit from. I have always wanted to inspire people in my community, especially women, because I knew they were subject to violence, discrimination, and immoral abuse in all forms things I never liked or accepted. Therefore, I decided to do something.

For example, I went to the market multiple times, bought clothes and sometimes sexy bras, and resold them to my classmates. Online sales were not as developed as they are now, so I had to do it this way to make more money. Another time, I sold pies made with either beef or fish, and it was all good.

I grew up in a very small, very poor town where the future of kids was problematic and uncertain. Leftover food was sometimes served as breakfast. With my brothers, we would sometimes walk long distances to school because my parents could not afford a taxi for all of us every day. As you know, school buses did not exist at that time, or were only available for kindergarten. It was painful and hurtful to see other kids being dropped off at school by their private drivers while we were walking. But the love and kindness my parents gave us were priceless. I believe that is one of the best things I inherited from them.

Of course, I had more pressure than others because I was the eldest. I had a brilliant childhood full of joy and happiness, despite not always having the things I wanted. I could play in the rain, soccer with the boys sometimes, or tennis. My parents made sure to give us the best they had and taught us to appreciate and love what we had at the moment.

I went to high school, then college, and graduated with a Bachelor's degree in Nursing. Dating was very hard living in that town. I remember being mocked at school several times, which was very frustrating and humiliating. I was ashamed of my body; I was curvy, and all my friends and cousins were skinny. Being a skinny girl at that time was so popular, unlike today where curvy girls are celebrated or solicited to the point that some undergo plastic surgery to get what I have naturally.

Despite being intelligent, graceful, kind, and beautiful, it was not enough for certain families to accept me for their sons. I remember one day, I was introduced to a guy by his aunt, who knew my parents and thought I would be a good fit for their nephew. The guy worked in finance and was living in the political capital, while I was living in the economic capital.

We liked each other and communicated often through phones until, one day, I could not get any text messages or phone calls from him. I was speechless and confused, blaming myself for what I had done to him to experience this. My sister-in-law was quiet; his aunt, who introduced us, was quiet. Six months later, after a work meeting, I met a mutual friend who told me about my finance guy's trip to Canada and that he had married a girl his family found better than me. The girl was a nurse, and her family was from a middle-class society.

At that moment, I choked up and didn't say anything. I just could not believe what I had just heard after blaming myself all that time for no reason. I was hurt and never looked back again. His marriage only lasted a year, and he wanted to come back to me, but it was too late because I had moved on.

I was working on the side as a hostess for events. One day, during a tourist event, I was selected to present a bouquet of flowers to the state representative. There were many high-profile figures and international guests in attendance.

Everything went well. I was dressed in a long black evening dress with a big green necklace covering my long neck. I wore a beautiful ponytail and long heels to enhance my elegance and charm.

I was approached by a tall guy, about six feet five inches tall. I had never seen him before. He introduced himself and asked for my name.

"My name is Poupy Gaelle," I said. "And you?" I asked.

He replied, "My name is Bassa."

"Nice to meet you," I replied with a warm smile.

"Nice to meet you too," he said.

He told me he was an international soccer player but also played for our national team. I did not believe him and thought he was just bragging. Of course, he was elegant, well-dressed, and his cologne smelled expensive, but I was still not convinced. He noticed that I was not impressed and asked me about myself. I told him.

He was rushing to leave and asked for my number. I was a little skeptical but ended up giving it to him. He said, "I will call you later." A luxury car stopped to pick him up, and I thought, *Hmmm...* and said to myself, *Anyway.*

The next day, around 4 p.m., I was taking a nap when my phone suddenly rang. It rang once or twice, and I picked up.

"Hey Poupy, how are you doing?" he said. "It's Bassa from yesterday. You remember?"

I said, "Oh yes, I remember you. I'm doing great, and you?"

He replied, "I'm okay," and added, "I'm on my way back to town. That is why I was rushing to leave yesterday."

I was like, *Hmmm, okay!*

He said, "Did you check my name out?"

I replied, "No," because I thought he was lying to me.

He said, "Wait a minute." He googled himself and sent me the results, including a picture of him with the national team and other international players. At that moment, I was impressed and thought, *Woah!* I did not say anything.

"Do you believe me now?" he asked.

Ironically, I replied, "Yes, I do believe you now."

Then he asked me, "Where do you live? I want to come see you now. I want to surprise you."

To be honest, I did not want to tell him because I was scared he might hang up after hearing the name of the street. I hesitated but finally spelled it out: "Bepanda?" It was known for being one of the poorest streets in my city.

To my big surprise, he did not mind and asked for the exact location so his driver could find the place. An hour later, he called again, saying he was there. I thought it was a joke. Thankfully, I was already showered. I changed into a cute dress, fixed my hair, put on soft makeup and sandals, and went out to see him.

When I arrived at the exact location, which was a five-minute walk from where I lived, he was there chatting with strangers. When he saw me, oh gosh, he smiled, ran toward me, and held me. I was joyful but so ashamed. He could not stop looking at me and talking. His driver stood behind him, just looking at him as if to say, *What is going on here?* but he ended up laughing, too.

We decided to have a drink at the closest bar facing us. Unfortunately, I do not drink alcohol, so I ordered natural juice, and he drank water, I believe. I asked him a little about himself as a way to get to know him better. He was having fun until his cousin called him.

He picked up the phone and told his cousin where he was.

"You are at Bepanda?" his cousin said. "What are you doing there?"

He replied, "I'm with Poupy Gaelle. You will get a chance to meet her soon, too." He said to his cousin, "Listen, I will give you a call back."

While we were talking, the bartender recognized him, came over, and asked if he was the one who played for the national team.

"Yes, that's me," he replied. They shook hands, and the bartender greeted him for coming.

After an hour there, they both decided to walk me home before they left. I was so embarrassed and ashamed of that place. Despite the fact that we had a big house with everything in it, it was not located in a comfortable or residential area.

He did not care at the beginning, but he was influenced by his cousin and friends later, which made the relationship unhealthy.

On our way home, he was perfectly fine talking, being funny. Finally, we got home. Only my mom was there, and she had no idea who he was. I introduced him to my mom; she greeted him and his driver. I was so embarrassed because I had never introduced a guy like that to my mom before. In our tradition, it is usually your fiancé that you present to your mom or dad.

She offered them whisky, but since they did not drink, they preferred water, which I gave them immediately. After a couple of minutes, they decided to leave. He asked me not to worry about them because all they wanted was to walk me safely home. He promised to call me as soon as he got home, which he did.

I thought after this, he would delete my number, but he did not. We kept in touch, and he promised to change my life and even where I lived. I was so happy and believed him at the moment.

The next day, he called me again and asked what I was doing. I was an intern at the hospital, so I told him that I was almost done with work. He asked me if I could come see him at a bistro located in the center of the city, Akwa. I replied, "No problem," but I wanted to go home first to shower and change.

At around 7 p.m., I met them at the bistro. He was there with his driver and his cousin, who had called him the day before. I greeted them, and then he introduced me to his cousin. We laughed about what had happened the day before. We ordered chocolate ice cream, burgers, fruits, tea, and fruit juice. We had a good time, and at 10 p.m., I told him I needed to go. He asked his driver to safely drive me home, which he did.

We kept in touch and became really good friends. He had a luxurious life and very important friends, and he introduced me to some of them. I noticed his driver always wanted to protect me and say things that would open my mind. I did not really pay attention until one day I discovered he was living with his baby mama and they had two or three kids together.

I got upset and decided never to see him again. I also did not want to live his type of life, knowing I could not afford it. He said he had not wanted me to know because he knew I would not accept hanging out with him, which was true. I started distancing myself from him.

Nothing ever happened between us. We never had sex or were in any very uncomfortable situation. It is true I kissed him multiple times, but nothing more, especially after finding out about his baby mama.

He also introduced me to his big brother, who owns a restaurant in Akwa. He was making me feel special, but I was not into it anymore. Also, he never kept his promise of changing my life. It was just hanging out all the time nothing really special, no car, no house, nothing that would make me say, "Wow, because of you I am now this."

Finally, he helped me find a good job at his friend's company. But I needed money to get new clothes and shoes because it was office work, and he kept promising me nothing. Thankfully, I was still working as a hostess for events, which provided extra money.

After working there for a couple of months, they really appreciated how fast I learned, my work ethic, my discipline, and my punctuality. But unfortunately, I did not get along with his friend's wife, who also worked in the same office with us.

For example, she would come in one day and send me to a cleaner on the corner of the street to drop off our boss's dirty clothes to wash. I did it the first time, and I did it the second time, but it became a habit for her. She would often mistake home for work. It was hard to handle until one day I got a new job at an insurance company and resigned.

I let Bassa know about my departure. I did not want to cause trouble between him and his friend, but to my surprise, he said, "Everybody knows about his friend's wife; she is difficult to deal with. I just did not want to let you know because I knew you needed better."

I thanked him for that, and we never spoke or saw each other again until one day I gave him a phone call from the U.S.A. He was surprised and happy for me at the same time, but I noticed an embarrassment in him, knowing that I was there not because of him but through my own effort. I also made sure to call his driver, who was also so happy for me.

Chapter 2: Life in the USA

I left my country, Cameroon, for the US when I was very young, between 28 and 29 years old, and I have lived here by myself ever since. All my family is back home in Africa, and I work hard and fight to help them improve their living conditions.

When I arrived in the US, my first impression at the airport was, *Woah!* It was huge, with travelers from everywhere. I was impressed by the skyscrapers in every city, the lighting, the water it was another world. I was speechless. Like every newcomer, I wanted to see Beyoncé, Kim Kardashian, Oprah, Michelle Obama, and other celebrities. I thought you could just see them like it showed on TV.

I saw diversity: Black, White, Asian, Latino, and Indian people that you rarely see on the street or at work in Africa. There were malls everywhere, coffee shops, fast-food restaurants, and bars. Buses and metros were seen on every corner. Expensive cars drove all over, but there were rarely taxis like back home.

But what kept my attention the most was that there were homeless people everywhere some with barely any clothes on, others screaming and walking without any exact direction. When I saw some White and Asian people among those groups, I was like, *Really?* Then I said, *Never mind.*

I was impressed by the big houses, mansions, the shape of apartments, beaches, and the interior design of some companies. The width of each highway, the stop signs, and the traffic signals on the road made me question my poor country! I believe everyone from Africa, especially the sub-Saharan part, would have felt the same. Really, no shade. Everything was clean and beautiful.

But I had a hard time with food. I remember one day my friends took me to lunch at McDonald's. It was my first time, and I did not know what to get. They had double burgers with large fries and drinks. I ordered a regular burger, large fries, and a drink. I got a Sprite, and they got Coca-Cola. When the order came, I enjoyed it, and I was expecting a real meal. They laughed so hard at me, saying we did not have that here. Honestly, I was confused but ended up making my own meals at home sometimes.

I found snacks too salty or too sweet sometimes, which explains the shape of certain people on the street. People talking faster made me almost want to cry sometimes no, I'm joking. I had a hard time communicating with people; I was struggling with the English language, which was a huge barrier for me. I could barely say a sentence in English. I am a French speaker, so you can understand what I am saying.

After getting my legal work permit and my Social Security Number, I thought about using my beautiful and smart personality to make a profit. This is how I started doing photo modeling, which gave me a couple of dollars to put in my pocket and buy myself what I wanted.

Nevertheless, I was confronted with unsolicited offers by some producers. For example, I had a photographer friend who invited me to come with him to a production studio so he could introduce me to the people he worked with. Once at the studio, I noticed that it was a music studio. He introduced me to the main producer and others. He told him what I was doing and what I planned to do here in Los Angeles.

He asked me if I had a headshot, and I said yes. He then asked me if I had a social media platform, and I said yes. He looked at my page and said I looked too serious that I must change my look to attract more views and get more work in the industry. He turned his head and showed me the other side of the wall, which had pictures of some rappers like Cardi B, Nicki Minaj, and Megan Thee Stallion.

I was like, "No, I'm not a musician, so I can't do that."

Then he said, "So forget about working if you can't do a certain style."

I felt uncomfortable and told my friend that I wanted to leave. On our way, he convinced me that the producer was right that I had to change my style. He offered to take a couple of pictures just to see how it looked.

We were in downtown at that moment. We went to the fashion district, where he bought some sexy clothes for the shoot. Once we were done, we shot a couple of pictures with different outfits in different places. After that, he edited them and sent them to me, which I also posted on my Instagram. Some looked good, but others were a little extravagant. I did not recognize myself in them, so I never spoke to him or saw any of them again.

I decided to do things my own way: to be my own manager, my own agent because I did not have one, and finally, my own publicist.

Also, I was offered $20,000 to play a sex worker in front of a camera by a Haitian producer who was ready to fly his crew to Los Angeles to film me. I declined and will never accept a role I would be uncomfortable playing. I was introduced to that person by a man I used to work for in his salon as a braider. He insisted and told me that it would be a good beginning for my acting career. I said no, blocked his number, and never spoke to him again.

For people aspiring to work in the entertainment industry, there are both good and bad propositions. It is your choice to select which one works best for you. Be careful with any contract you sign because what is done in the dark will always come to the light.

Then, a couple of weeks after, I took acting classes and quickly signed with a talent agency. I remember lining up at 4 a.m. with my friend Baron, who had come earlier at 3:45 a.m. to pick me up for Central Casting. Once we got there, we were tenth in line; people were already there waiting, some with small blankets, others with their coffee. It was cold and unbelievable. But in the end, it pays off because later on we were registered, and I was sent on set in Hollywood multiple times for background work.

This also gave me enough money to buy myself everything I wanted without reaching out to any man or anyone else, but it was not enough to pay my bills such as rent, electricity, phone bills, and to make a living from it. Then I decided to go back to school so I could get a degree, earn more money, and live a better life with a career.

At first, I thought it was the best idea ever, but it was just a utopia. Because the degree I was chasing and the work afterward were two very different things.

So I registered in 2018 as a first-year college student. Imagine a girl from a poor city in Cameroon now in Los Angeles, California. For me, it was unbelievable; it was like a dream come true. At first, I did not really know what to study, so I started with justice administration.

My journey in school was so funny. Sometimes I had no idea what my professor was talking about. Despite the fact that I asked her a lot of questions, I still could not relate. I looked at myself sometimes and was convinced I would never be a good investigator or anything like that. I was sure I was lying to myself while taking that class. I left after just one semester.

I left for two reasons. Classes were remotely converted to online classes due to the COVID-19 pandemic, and it was so hard to take classes online, especially because I was not used to manipulating computers and, more importantly, Canvas. It was so depressing and stressful that it made me drop the class and never take it again.

Then I started taking more English classes and mathematics until I met with a counselor with whom I had a very deep conversation about what I was planning to achieve. She asked me multiple questions about what I wanted, and I told her, "TV."

She said, "TV? What exactly?"

I replied, "Journalism." Because I knew I was already doing acting work and it was so hard to make a living from that. Doing this would allow me to stay in the same area for instance, I decided to get a journalism degree so I could still be around media and celebrities.

It was not easy at all. For example, the struggle to afford tuition every semester on one hand, and the struggle of paying bills on the other hand, was hurting me so hard. Sometimes I wanted to quit. I had to work two to three jobs to adjust my income. Sometimes I wanted to take a picture and send it back home to show how hard it was because everyone believes that since you live in the USA, you automatically have money based on what they see on E! News and other reality TV shows.

But while coming back late at night from work, looking at those homeless people sleeping on the floor made me cry and motivated me to work twice, even ten times harder, in order to make it.

It was hard, very hard, to the point that I was skipping some semesters instead of attending school so I could work and save a little bit of money. As an immigrant, unfortunately, I did not get loans and was not qualified for Government Financial Aid. On the side, I was doing small activities that could help add to my income, such as online clothing sales on Poshmark. I had an account on that platform where I was posting articles for sale, but the fact that it was a very competitive market also meant it was too slow and did not give me enough money to stay there.

I decided to open my own clothing line, which I called "SAPPEY BRANDS." "Sape" means "well dressed" in French, so for English speakers to spell it right, I added an additional "P" and "Y" at the end to avoid them saying "Sapee" with the sound "e" at the end of "ey." It was all cool. I started selling hoodies in all different colors such as white, black, red, gray, and blue, in different styles like full-zip and regular hoodies.

But unfortunately, with the COVID-19 pandemic, I lost everything. The merchandise I ordered online came in very bad quality materials. I was shocked and devastated. I remember the stimulus check that was sent to people helped me order a big quantity of merchandise, and the rest I sent to my parents back home to help them buy enough food and save it. I felt empty and broken at the same time bad merchandise, no more money. There are no words to describe how bad I felt at that moment; even crying did not help me. I was by myself no boyfriend, no support but I kept moving on.

I was also taking classes online and kept working at the same time as a security guard. I remember nobody wanted to work because of COVID-19, but I had no choice. I am an immigrant and needed money to afford a living but, more importantly, to support my family back home at that challenging moment. My parents contacted me and wanted me to rest to avoid contracting the virus, but unfortunately, I could not. It was not disobedience to them, but for those who live here in the USA, especially as an immigrant, you know what I am talking about.

Thankfully, I was able to do extra overtime work and save a lot, which helped me afford my tuition and also help my parents. I never had that much money since then.

During the same period, I published my first book called *All The Way To The Screen* and used a pen name, "LA DAME DE FER" (https://www.amazon.ca/ALL-WAY-SCREEN-Dame-Fer/dp/1664155783/).

That book was a failure because I made a lot of mistakes. Of course, it was my first experience as an author, and it was probably due to stress and other issues such as miscommunication between the publishing company and me. But hopefully, I learned from that and corrected it so next time it will not happen again. I wanted to make a movie version of it. I remember I handed some copies to friends and celebrities I met in the industry so they could either refer me to filmmakers and producers or help boost the sales, but it never happened.

I love working, being creative, and also adventurous. I am not scared to fail because I know it is part of a learning process. It sure brings you down but also prepares you to stand up fully prepared and ready to do better. Failure is not something you plan or order to happen; it comes by itself unexpectedly. It hurts really bad, to the point of making you want to quit or abandon anything you were working on, but you have to be strong enough and determined to make it happen.

In a short period of time, I lost my clothing line "Sappey Brands," did not have any success with my book, and lost all that money that never came back. But this did not stop me.

A year later, I noticed that the African community did not have a platform that could give them the opportunity to shoot their movies or express themselves, so I had the idea to fix that problem. That is how I opened a production company called "Equity Production Company." I invited my classmates to help me build that business by writing articles and publishing stories, but no one really reacted to my offer. I knew I had an amazing idea and was also talented, but it was still not enough because I could not do everything by myself. As an entrepreneur, you need people to assist you; otherwise, you will fail.

The next year, I started to feel bad about my career. I was told my voice did not sound like an American accent, so it was already a conflict that I needed to fix really fast. I was good at interviewing people, so I asked my professor if I could volunteer on the red carpet. It was a moment when everybody was scared of working because of the COVID-19 pandemic that killed millions of people, according to the CDC report, but I was more motivated than ever and took courage with both hands.

14

I started attending the red carpet as a volunteer each semester. Vaccination was mandated, and the card was highly recommended for any volunteer or workers at those events. So many events were canceled and closed, but the couple that started reopening again, slowly but surely, was very strict and cautious. Therefore, I had to get my two shots of Pfizer at CVS in Santa Monica.

The first red carpet event I attended was the "Writers and Illustrators of the Future" by L. Ron Hubbard, then the "LA Press Club Association," and then the "Hollywood Christmas Parade." Each semester I was doing that until it became flawless to me; it became like a game. I knew everything to do at each of them, such as setting up the red carpet on the floor, putting signs on the floor for photographers and media outlets to indicate their position at the event. I also ended up being great at checking people in, handling the prizes to winners during the ceremony, flowers, and even more.

Then I asked my professor if I could interview people on the red carpet for the school's newspaper, and she said, "Yes." It was a magic moment for me because I went from interviewing students on campus to celebrities on the red carpet in Hollywood. I was a little frustrated my first time; I was nervous and anxious at the same time but also very confident.

It was around 2:30 p.m. in the afternoon when I arrived at the red-carpet location on Vine Street in Hollywood. I was supposed to meet there with our school photographer and video producer, who was also in charge of bringing the school microphone and cameras for that special occasion. I showed up and I could not see her. She was inside the banquet. I tried to call her to know her position; she told me she was already there, and she came out. I was so happy to see her. You could tell by the big smile on my face. We were two, and I was more confident.

15

Then, when I asked her to give me a microphone so we could start practicing for the interview, she looked at me and said, "Which microphone?" I was surprised because I knew that the day before we were all on campus with the professor and did a rehearsal. We were each assigned a task for the next day, like who would do what once on the red carpet. To my big surprise, she had nothing but her camera to take photos. I was speechless and also humiliated. I was well dressed with nice makeup; I believe it was the moment I thought I could make a beautiful impression and get beautiful videos, but no.

I found another way to do the interview that day, and the only way to do it was through writing. I decided to write down everything each of those celebrities was saying. That form of interviewing is horrible, especially when you have multiple people in front of you. It can work for a single interview but not for a large audience like the red carpet. To be honest, it is the hardest thing to do because most of them speak too fast, and in the newspaper, you have to put the exact words of each person you have interviewed.

Also, on the red carpet, things go faster. You have to be brief while asking questions because the line is long, and people, especially A-list celebrities, need to come first and have space around to take pictures and interviews, so other people have to move in order to let other newcomers walk onto the red carpet and take pictures.

After the incident on the red carpet with my co-worker, that same night or the day after, she was supposed to send me unedited pictures, and she did not. I asked for photos of me a week after she took them that day, and she said she deleted them all because her memory card was full. I was mortified and furious. This time, not only had I lost the opportunity to have a video tape of myself interviewing celebrities on the red carpet in Hollywood, but now I had all my pictures deleted. Nothing would prove that I attended that red carpet event, my first big professional work.

The next month, I decided to take a photography class. During that class, the professor recommended each student have his or her own camera, so I ordered mine online, which I am still using today. I also bought my own microphone so now I could be prepared for the next red-carpet interview. I learned how to take photos, how to shoot videos, and now I was able to interview people on the red carpet easily. I built those skills with time, and now I can master them.

I was the best interviewer in my class something I did not know I would be able to do first because I was coming from Africa, and the second reason was because of my English-speaking barrier. I decided to create a platform where I could post all those red-carpet interviews so people could notice me. It is called "Africallywoodthshow," a 90-minute format program I created that aims to highlight African celebrities living and performing in Hollywood to connect with their public in Africa.

I believe this will help me do my own work and share it with the public because working for CNN, FOX NEWS, CBS, and others was not necessarily my dream. I wanted to develop that platform and hire people who are less represented and who have fewer chances for a job to perform there. People have no idea how hard it is because graduating is one thing and looking for a job after is another thing. So with that platform, I am sure I will have something to do and, more importantly, inspire others, which is a good idea, I believe.

Have you ever wondered what working on the red carpet as a journalist looks like? Please read this.

For almost three years, I have been covering the red carpet for different kinds of award celebrations. It is one of my biggest accomplishments since I moved to Los Angeles from Africa.

At first, the immensity and the luxury of the event and the place intimidate you to the point you ask yourself if it is real or if you will really be a part of it. You feel excited about it, especially when you know that celebrities and very important people will attend the same event particularly when it is your first time.

For example, my first experience was in Hollywood for the red carpet of "The Writers and Illustrators of the Future," which took place in a luxury ballroom of a celebrity hotel on Vine Street. It is in two steps: first, the posing and taking pictures of winners, nominees, and guests outside on the red carpet; then, the award ceremony inside the ballroom.

The sun was shining down on the town as usual at over 85 degrees that day. Unfortunately, you cannot do anything about it; you just keep working and being professional interviewing nominees, winners, and guests.

I was burning under my two-piece outfit, a beautiful yellow skirt and orange short-sleeve top I wore that day. I was gorgeous, simple, and elegant. Some people who attended the event asked me if I was a celebrity; it made me laugh and feel more confident at the same time. It was my first time being around such a talented and high-profile Hollywood family. The emotion is there but indescribable.

The second one I attended was in Hollywood during the Christmas Parade in November 2021. As you know, it is the winter season and it is very cold. The red carpet is outside, and there is no way to hide close to a chiminea (laugh) or a blanket to stay warm. No, sweetheart, you have to stay strong and get the best interview ever. Everyone wants to rush to get the best picture on the red carpet to go inside and stay warm; therefore, getting their attention is not easy at all.

Most celebrities come with their publicists; therefore, it is hard to get a picture with them or ask them for something you had in mind. "You are not here to take pictures or bother them, so keep moving," they will reply to you. You have to interview celebrities and get quotes for the school's newspaper. Therefore, you have to forget about the cold;

otherwise, you will miss it, and your presence there will be useless.

So far, I have covered five Hollywood Red Carpets, and believe me, as a Black woman from Africa, it is a huge deal a big accomplishment. A real dream comes true. Definitely my American dream!

I am very proud of myself today and wish to share more with you. For example:

How can you succeed in a beautiful interview on the red carpet?

There is no particular rule or code to interview people and celebrities on the red carpet based on my own experience. However, you have to be friendly, smiley, smart, fast, polite, and spray good energy or vibes; otherwise, nobody will come to you. The reality is that most of the celebrities and guests come on the red carpet to have fun and enjoy the moment, so in order for you to succeed in your interview on the red carpet, please follow these steps or do these things, and you will be fine:

- **First**, avoid asking them questions that will embarrass them or make them feel bad, especially those from gossip chats like cheating rumors, divorce, or anything that will put them in a bad light.
- **Second**, make it short and sweet because the line is long, and you might get stuck, preventing other people from moving on for an interview.
- **Third**, be polite, always smile, and make them feel comfortable around you. Give them compliments about their outfits, their hair (for ladies), shoes whatever can make them laugh and be happy.
- **Then**, always ask for their name, especially if they are not known by the public. First and last names are primordial for the after-work production or news writing.
- **Finally**, try to make connections or ask for referrals; that will help you in the future for your career.

So, here are a couple of pieces of advice I decided to share with you if you plan to cover the red carpet one day. These details are very important to learn because they do not teach that in school.

Chapter 3: Life After Graduation

So, I finally graduated on June 6, 2023, from Los Angeles City College, majoring in Journalism.

Poupy Gaelle graduation photo

I was so happy that finally I would be able to find a good job, earn great money, and start making a living from that. I was working at Ben & Jerry's, a national ice-cream shop, but it was paying only the minimum wage of $17/hr, which was so insignificant considering the inflation and the hard work behind it.

For example, we were serving ice cream, working as cashiers, providing customer service, doing dishwashing, and cleaning the whole store every night. I did not mind the tasks we had to do, but the pay was the true definition of a lot of work for low pay. Especially because tips were insignificant like $5, sometimes $8 or $10 maximum each day.

I was contacted by an Entertainment News company in Hollywood that wanted me to join their team. The main reason was that they needed a bilingual person, more importantly someone who could cover African stories and red carpets in Paris ("Cannes"). I was so excited about the offer that I decided to quit my job at Ben & Jerry's to follow my passion and start a new, well-paying job two weeks after the announcement. Knowing I would start working with the new employer, but I was wrong.

They did not make the announcement they had shared with me through email. In addition, I was never called to start work or to sign a contract. I was choked and humiliated. I could not wait to start that job. Maybe it was my mistake to trust so fast or believe people just like that? I am still looking for the answer. Or I was just so excited to know that I would finally be able to start making money from my new work based on my degree.

During the same period, I was having trouble with my new roommates. I ended up suing them for abuse and discrimination over a dog bite situation. Previously, here is what happened: I broke up with my boyfriend and was looking for a new place to stay. This is how those new roommates offered me a place to stay. Later on, we ended up in court.

So here is what really happened: I was dating this guy, a Black African American man, not a celebrity. He was 52 years old, six feet five inches tall, single but with grandkids. We met at work. I know he could have been my daddy, but I was in love. He was one of the supervisors, and I was a simple employee; we were working on different floors. He was on the 8th floor, and I was on the 4th floor.

One day, we all met in front of the clocking machine. He heard me talking and noticed that I have an accent, so he asked me where I was from. I told him, and since then he never removed his eyes from me. He came to my floor to check things for no reason; he checked on me in the break room sometimes. This is how we connected and kept in touch.

I was a little skeptical about this whole situation because I always promised myself not to date a colleague. After three months, I finally decided to go on a date with him. Everything went well. He invited me to his place, a one-bedroom apartment, which I agreed to. The relationship was going well to the point he brought me to his church, then introduced me to his pastor, and then to the whole congregation as a new member.

I moved to his place. Every morning I was waking up earlier to make breakfast; he was so happy and also loved my cooking. I remember one day I made avocado with a baguette (French bread). He enjoyed it to the point he called his best friend to brag about it. I could not stop laughing.

Things started to go bad between us when I quit that job and found a new one in Hollywood not only was it going to pay me more, but it also offered a new environment and new opportunities. He got jealous and was very rude to me for no reason.

I remember one day I told him I was going shopping; I needed new jeans, tennis shoes, and new shirts for my new job. He started talking about how I was going to leave him once I started the other job, which was false. A few weeks later, I finally started my new job, and I liked it.

It was customer service at a luxury fitness club in Hollywood where the membership was $350 a month. It was really fancy, only for rich people and celebrities in particular. The first two weeks of work were for training before the real work began. There was a lot to learn about the new job, the location, its access, and other details.

It was really far from where I was living, so only Uber helped me get to work quickly, and I used public transportation after work, but sometimes Uber too because I was on the closing shift. He never had time to give me a ride to work or to come pick me up, which was fine; I had my money and could afford Uber every day.

One weekend, we went to the hospital to visit his dad, who was hospitalized. This is how he introduced me to his mom and little brother. We checked in at the front desk of the hospital and went upstairs to see his dad. He introduced me to his dad, too. The connection went well. His dad was lying down in the bed and could not walk; he had just had surgery.

There was a basketball game playing on the TV in his dad's bedroom. For some reason, they started to argue. I was lost and did not know what to do. I left them going back and forth. I was so uncomfortable, but *hélas!* In less than half an hour, he said we had to go. After answering all his dad's questions, I was happy to meet him and know that he was okay.

We finally left. On our way home, he stopped at a grocery store. I thought he was going to get something from there. He came back to the car and asked me to come with him. We went into the store, and a very young lady, about 20 to 23 years old, came to me. He introduced me to her. I asked who she was, and he replied, "This is my goddaughter." I shook her hand and smiled at her, and she did the same with me. Then we left and went to another store where he bought himself new shirts and jeans.

He joked while asking me for my credit card to pay his bills. Ironically, I said no. He checked out, and we left.

Tension started to be noticeable between us for no reason. I started to feel bad. I talked about it to a friend, and she asked me to leave that place that I did not have to stay there.

The next day was Monday. I went to work, and I heard one coworker saying that he was leaving the state for another one where his parents live. That news came to me as a gift.

24

I approached him when he was alone and asked if I could get his spot where he lives, and he said no problem. I just had to ask the other girls because they all lived together, which I did, and they said yes.

But the problem was that he was scheduled to leave in two months, which was a nightmare for me. The relationship was degrading slowly and slowly, and I could not handle it anymore.

I woke up the next day and wanted to make breakfast as usual, and he said no; he was not going to eat eggs or drink coffee. Instead, he made himself oatmeal for the first time we were together. Then the other day, I came back from work and made a fabulous dinner: rice with sautéed salmon and sautéed chicken in two different sauces, which he highly appreciated.

The next day, before going to work, I cooked rice so he could eat it with the other sauce he had not touched. Surprisingly, he texted me at work and asked me why I cooked the white rice again. I said, "Is there a problem with the rice? I also made a sweet potato that you can eat." He replied to me that I should have cooked the brown rice instead. He did not touch it.

The next day, I made a salad like hors d'oeuvres, but he did not eat it. He started to be aggressive for no reason; everything was now a problem for him. I forgot to mention that on top of that, I was a student; I was taking classes online. So just imagine! I was mentally affected and was feeling really bad.

First, I noticed his goddaughter was more and more present at home, which was not the case before. I did not say anything. One weekend, on Sunday to be specific, she came home. I was in the bedroom doing my homework; they were in the living room playing games, then watching movies together. After three hours of working, I decided to go for a walk.

Five minutes later, she called me. I did not pick up the phone. Then 30 minutes after, he called me; I was at CVS to get some feminine hygiene products and other personal items. He called; I picked up the phone, and he asked me where I was, and I told him. He started to scream at me like a child and told me his goddaughter called me and wanted braids and I did not reply. It was very uncomfortable and unbelievable.

I asked him to remain calm as I was coming back home. Once I got home, he was gone with her. A few minutes later, he came back. We had an argument, and he called her on a video call and allowed her to disrespect me, which I did not agree with. Then he asked me to leave his house. It was around 9 p.m., and I had no idea where to go.

I contacted my friend and explained the situation. She texted me the address of the hostel she used to live in, so I immediately booked a night and called Uber to come pick up my stuff. He thought I was playing, so I packed everything and left. It was a nightmare for me. I could not sleep. Not only was the place not agreeable or even comfortable, I had no choice that night. It was in the hood. I stayed there until the new place was finally available.

We were coworkers but also friends. So one day, one of the girls invited me for a tour of the apartment, which I did. Everything was great. She had a dog but told me it was not a problem because they always kept him on the balcony. Regarding the paperwork, she told me not to worry because they would take care of that.

The next day, I went on a date with a guy I met at the gym. As a front desk and customer service employee, I was talking to everybody, and people really liked me for my smile, good customer service skills, and the positive energy I was spraying good vibes in the group.

My new job at a fitness club center, a fancy place where celebrities and wealthy people come to exercise.

I was hired as a front desk and customer service worker who would be there to check in members and assist others. I was in contact with guests all the time and was so confident, and the satisfaction was there. I knew my job very well **but ended up resigning from this fabulous job because of the manager's bad behavior.**

What happened is that one day, I was scheduled to work on the red carpet and was also off at work, so there was no problem for me. I got there at 1 p.m., helped set up the red carpet on the floor, put the signs up, checked people in, and later introduced celebrities to photographers and then to TV for an interview.

So I met this Black actor from *General Hospital*. I greeted him, then wrote his name on the small board I was holding, and then introduced him to photographers and then to network TV for an interview. He really appreciated my service that night and agreed to take a picture with me that I shared later with my followers. He liked the picture and commented under the post:

"Thank you so much, you were great," and added a flower emoji, which was very kind of him.

The next day at work, everybody commented on that post asking me who he was, including my manager, who had a crush on him. She is a German single lady with a mixed boy; her baby daddy is a Black American, and she confessed she liked tall Black men. So she asked me to invite him to the gym so she could give him a tour and connect better with him.

I replied to her that I did not know him personally like she thinks. She insisted, and at first, I did not find it professional. Secondly, I thought that if it were me inviting someone I know, they would have said I violated company policy, and now for her, I have to do that?

Since then, she started making my life difficult at work with unfounded accusations, unfair treatment, and other issues to the point that one day, she posted in the group chat:

"We are looking for a missing package that was designated for the spa. Has any of you seen it?"

I was on a night shift, which means I was not at work yet because I was scheduled for 3 p.m. to 11:30 p.m., and it was the morning she texted. My coworker I worked with the night before did not say anything or reply to the text message. I replied and said:

"Please ask Perez, the duty manager, who took that package and said he was going to give it to the spa manager. We saw him take the package."

My co-worker still had not said anything to confirm that what I was saying was true.

Then I added:

"There are cameras, so it's easy to just review them and see who received it and find out."

She replied that, "Now every package will go to the valet, and that is the last time we look for packages here."

I was offended and felt insulted by her comment, even though I knew I did not take it and never did things like that. Fifteen minutes later, another front desk worker on the morning shift texted in the group chat:

"Hey, I just found the package; it was under the desk."

I was glad not only that someone else found it but also that I was not even at work, so they could not say I just put it back. I was expecting an apology from her, but she never did. I was expecting the other coworker I worked with that night to say something, but she never did.

I took it easy and went to work that day. It was very cold between us. I knew I did not want to work there anymore. The whole shift felt so long; I thought it would never end. It was the same week as payday. I waited until I received my direct deposit, and the next day early morning, I sent her my resignation letter, which took effect the same day. For me, it was over. I was gone and would never accept that kind of injustice.

The others wondered why I resigned, but she knew. I never said what happened between her and me to cause that. I felt free, probably jobless at that moment, but totally confident that sometimes you have to make people respect you instead.

Fitness Club Lobby photo by Poupy Gaelle Nguetsop
The club is located in Hollywood, close to the shopping mall but very discreet from the public. The membership costs $350 per month with a year contract and does not include personal trainer costs or the spa. So it is very expensive and not affordable for regular people.

So, I like flirting, and one day, a guest came and wanted a tour. There were two of us at the front desk, and I decided to do the tour. While doing the tour, we were required to ask questions to better understand the customer's needs. So, when I asked the guy, he said he was a lawyer and was looking for a co-working place so he could often work there quietly. He was short, like 5'5" tall, Hispanic, very attractive, and polite. We toured, and everything went very well to the point he gave positive feedback to the management team about me. It was a good move and a win for me that day.

Every time the guy showed up at the gym, I was flirting with him. Every time, until one day, he noticed that and stopped by me during his check-in and said:

"Please, can you check my husband's profile? I want to know if his account is already active or not."

I remained silent for a moment and said to myself, *A husband?*

Please do not blame me for that; I am from Africa and not used to gay people.

I asked him his husband's name so I could look it up. He gave me his husband's name, and I found out the guy was also a good-looking lawyer as well. I could not believe it. I was speechless and shared the story with one of my co-workers, who could not stop laughing. It was very funny and sad at the same time. I had no idea he was gay.

Four months later, there were very nice guys coming to the club, like movie actors, TV personalities, public figures, and musicians who were very wealthy and attractive as well. Unfortunately, pictures with them were not allowed.

One day, while putting towels on different levels so members could use them, one of the members I admire came to me and asked if I liked the concert, and I replied yes. He said:

"We are Wednesday, and the concert is Friday. Will you be able to attend?"

We follow each other on social media, which facilitates our communication. However, Habib mentioned that there would be a couple and a friend of his joining us at that concert. I did not have any problem with that. I thought it was a way for him to introduce me to his friends. Late at night, he sent me details from Instagram, and we kept in touch. We kept in touch and were communicating until that special day.

Friday arrives, and I could not wait to see him. I went shopping early that day and bought new white boots and a new wig to wear. I did my nails and also got a new small handbag that would match my jacket. The concert was set to start at 7 p.m., but he wanted us to be there by 7:30 p.m. or 8 p.m.

I started getting ready and was a little confused about what to wear that night. It was my first time attending a concert in

31

Los Angeles. I finally decided to dress up for the occasion: I wore black jeans, a black bodysuit, a white leather jacket on top, and a black small handbag to carry my phone and lipstick.

Once at the entrance, I gave him a phone call to notify him that I was already there. He came to the front entrance to pick me up. We were both so happy to see each other, and we hugged, and he said:

"Wow, you dressed up! I like it."

I smiled at him and thanked him for the compliment.

He invited me to have a drink, but unfortunately, I do not consume alcohol or beer. So I got a strawberry juice, and we went inside where a huge crowd was enjoying music while waiting for the main artist scheduled for that night to come and perform. We were talking, laughing, and enjoying that moment together until he received a phone call from one of his friends who said he was coming to join us.

He asked for a couple of minutes so he could go pick up his friend at the front entrance. Once his friend came, he introduced him to me, and it was very cool. His name was Martino, originally from Italy. Very tall and handsome, six feet four with an athletic shape. He wore short jeans, a white shirt, and tennis shoes. He was an artist (painter).

They had a good time at the event, dancing, chanting, recording short videos, and taking pictures. We left for a juice bar to get something to drink and eat. We got popcorn and drinks. Antonio paid for himself while Habib paid for both of us.

When we went back to the concert room, the more we were enjoying the music, the more both guys were getting too close to each other. I was surprised and confused. Both guys started hugging and touching like a couple.

"I was confused and speechless at the same time."

"I did not know if I came for him or if it was just an invitation?"

Both guys were enjoying the moment, and you could tell they were a real gay couple. During all the time spent with them, he did not kiss me, touch me, or make me feel like it was a romantic date between us.

The concert ended, and everybody left. We all met outside and were happy to have attended the event. There were couples outside close to us, and I noticed that one of the couples was one of the fitness trainers from the same club I work at. We looked at each other and said hello. The trainer introduced his friend as his partner to us, so they were also a gay couple who came to enjoy the concert.

After that, Habib's friend left with his car. I ordered an Uber and left, too. No kiss, nothing that could tell that it was a romantic date between Habib and me. When I got home, I texted him and notified him that I was safely home. He replied he was glad to hear that, and we wished each other good night.

The next day, I went to work and shared the story with my co-worker, who also could not wait to hear from me. When I told her the story, she started laughing at me again. She said:

"I knew he was gay but just did not want to discourage you."

She is from here, and they are better at knowing these things. I had no idea and was blind, just going on a date. Anyway, it was a beautiful experience and a great night with different people. I learned from there and now pay more attention to the people I talk to or go on dates with.

Dating in Los Angeles is very difficult because most of the guys in this area are gay, which means they look good for other guys, and therefore women struggle to find a good match. Another thing is that guys with wives or girlfriends are sometimes gay, too, because of pressure from society and the regard of others; they try to cover it by having girls by their side. Multiple situations like that have been seen at the club and even at the workplace.

It goes both ways with girls, too. There are so many of them who are lesbians, but with the stigma of society and the judgment of other people toward them, some prefer to remain quiet about it while others are open in public. But this situation is seen more on the men's side than women's.

On November 17, I finally moved in. My new roommate asked me not to use the front door entrance, so we used the back instead. She told me I would not have access to the gym or the patio. I did not know why, but whatever I did not care about it. So, because the month was already ending, I sent her half of the rent. She sent it back to me and said they would not charge me for that month; instead, I should pay at the beginning of the new month, which was December 1st.

Everything was good; we were all on good terms. We spent Thanksgiving together, then celebrated my birthday a couple of days after. Until one day, it was on December 9, 2022, when my roommate brought a dog into our room. I was in a Zoom meeting for class and was not paying attention. The dog jumped on me and bit me on my right arm and scratched me on my left arm. I was screaming so loud, pushed him far away, and escaped from that room to the next room. I was screaming and in emotional distress. The other girl came and helped me calm down.

The dog owner and other girls were in the living room, and none of them called 911 or paramedics to assist me medically. After five to ten minutes of silence, I decided to go take a shower and left the house for a graduation ceremony at school. Then later, I went to the urgent care but left because I did not have insurance.

A couple of weeks later, after waiting for the dog owner to provide medical assistance and compensation for the injury for a week, I finally decided to go to the urgent care center, where I received a shot of vaccine and antibiotics for my wound. I paid all medical bill expenses from my own pocket. When I got home, they served me an eviction notice and never notified either the building management or the insurance company to assist me.

Many cases like this have been reported concerning African immigrants, and everything has been silent until now.

I texted the dog owner to provide proof of her dog's vaccination and confirmation if she had notified the building management so I could get assistance.

She replied, "I will talk to my lawyer and will get back to you," the dog owner said.

I left home for work at 8 a.m., and once I was back home at 6 p.m., all my belongings were outside, and there was a written notice on the door: "Leave the keys under the door." I was shocked.

I put my key in, and it did not open the door. I took a picture of the locked door and my belongings on the floor, and I went downstairs to call the police. It was very cold, and my jacket was not heavy enough to keep me warm. It took two to three hours for the police to get there because they said it was a civil matter, so it was not an emergency.

Once they arrived, I explained the situation to them. In addition, I showed them the eviction notice the girls had given me before we went upstairs to the third floor where our apartment was located. The police asked for my keys, tried to open the door themselves, and it did not open. They knocked on the door; no one answered three times. You could hear the dog barking inside the apartment, which indicated the owner and others were there.

The police knocked again for the fourth time, and finally, Amia, who collected the rent and who had sent the eviction notice who was also like the spokesperson for the apartment came out. She shared her side of the story in her favor, of course. She was white and wanted to make me feel guilty and like a bad person in front of the two officers. The dog owner was a Black American who decided not to come out because they knew what they were doing by sending a white girl to talk.

But when the police asked her about the eviction notice, she acknowledged she had sent it, and the police told her it was wrong what they were doing to me and that it was illegal because:

"In the notice, it said to be out by January 1st, 2023, and we are December 22nd, 2022, which is not okay and is illegal," the police said.

The police fixed the situation that night and let me go in until the eviction notice took effect.

During the last couple of weeks, it was tense between us. I decided not to talk to them anymore. I was hurt and betrayed by the people I was living with.

The next day, I tried to contact the building management myself and notified them about the incident and the recent eviction by my roommates. The building management replied and let me know that the whole unit was already jeopardized and asked me which insurance I had contacted. I did not know any. The building management replied to me and listed company insurances listed on the building lease but also told me that each unit has its own insurance company, such as Assurant, Lemonade, or State Farm. They expected the roommates to share it with me, but unfortunately, they did not.

For instance, the building management also found out I was not even registered on the lease, as I had been told by my roommates in the beginning. So, they collected my rent, then kicked me out after using my money, knowing full well what they were doing. They were subleasing and had exceeded the maximum number of guests. So I was a victim.

On December 30th, 2022, I packed my stuff and left for the hostel. No medical assistance, no compensation, no insurance name communicated to me so I could get help. This is how racist and discriminatory African immigrants are treated in America! Unfortunately.

A couple of weeks later, I contacted a law firm to help fight for my case. But after three months, because of a lack of collaboration with that law firm, and because the dog owner still refused to communicate her dog's insurance company name, my case was dropped by that company.

Determined to go further, I decided to file a small claim by myself for $10,000.00. I know it was insignificant compared to what the state requires. I did not have a lawyer and decided to represent myself. The court date was scheduled, and I just waited for them to appear in court.

But while waiting for the court date, a TV show contacted me to share my story, and in exchange, they would help me collect the judgment if I won. Because there is no guarantee that the defendant is going to pay the judgment if they lose the case, which I agreed to. Also, $500 for participation was added to the contract. Both parties agreed (the TV show production and the victim).

I shared my part of the story with the producer with all evidence. The date of the court arrived; I went to the court, and the defendant was not there. As a motive, they said they were not served; therefore, a new initial date was set up for another one month ahead a deal that was made by the production and the victim in order for them to serve the defendant. I naively believed them, ignoring that once I appeared on the show, the other court hearing would be canceled and invalid anymore.

So, the day of the TV show, I woke up earlier, took a shower, and got dressed up. I put on makeup, got my hair done, and was ready for the camera. The production sent a car to pick me up at the production location. I was confident and remained calm and very concentrated.

Once at the production, the check-in process started: ID card check-in, name tag on, and I was directed to my dressing room. A couple of minutes later, another lady came out for contract signing and other agreements between the production and me, the victim. Then, I went back to my dressing room.

After that, the assistant producer came over with the whole story printed for rehearsal. I was offered drinks, coffee, and snacks while waiting. And then, I was called for a makeup last retouch by the production team. Everything went well, and now it was my hair. The producer came over, talked to me about everything, asked me to be myself and to share the story as it is. To not be afraid, I respectfully said yes, and together we left my dressing room for the main studio.

Once at the studio, it was a waiting place where participants could sit while waiting to be called by the sheriff to enter the big room. There was also a journalist there in charge of interviewing all participants at the end of the hearing show. Devices like microphones were put on each of us for better communication and good sound. A sound check was done two to three times before the final moment.

For a minute, everything was silent, and I, the victim, was called to the courtroom. Then the defendant came with the white girl, so there were two against me. Then the judge made her appearance in the court.

She started with the victim by asking my full name, where I live, how I met the defendant, and what really happened. It was all okay, as I also presented all evidence to the jury. Of course, it was a TV show, but on the other hand, as the victim, I wanted justice, as I was suffering from my injuries.

But unfortunately, the judge seemed to be partial and insensitive to my pain. At a moment, I became emotional; I was hurt, betrayed by people I believed were my friends, and now by the justice system. When I realized that not only was the judge rude to me, but she also minimized my pain and gave reason to the defendant, who used so many lies during the hearing to defend herself, I was devastated.

When the judge closed the hearing, I found out I lost my case but hoped I would win the other one previously scheduled. I left the show crying. Just outside the court, the journalist standing there started his interview. When I was asked during the interview if it was just about the money, I replied, "No! It wasn't."

The whole crew was trying to put emphasis on the money I asked for in my case more than what really happened. How can people possibly just focus on money, ignoring the pain, the emotional distress I was going through, but more importantly, the injustice I faced not only for being evicted but also for not being compensated as the law requires?

It was a brutal injustice. Once again, after that scene, it just demonstrated how African immigrants are mistreated and discriminated against, and no action follows. I was driven back by a crew member to my workplace in Hollywood. It was very bad for me the rest of the day.

A couple of weeks later, the initial court date arrived. I showed up, and one thing kept my attention: my name was not listed at the front door for the people whose hearing was scheduled. I thought it was a mistake. When the court opened, the check-in list was made, and I did not hear my name, so I notified the lady. She checked my name and did a second check and found out my case was dismissed.

Confused, I asked why? They said I did that, and I had no idea what was going on. Then the sheriff asked me to follow him outside so we could figure out what was happening. Once outside, the officer asked me if I went on the computer and canceled my case, and I replied, "No." But I remembered about the TV show hearing and shared it with the officer, and from there he explained to me that once you go there, it is final; you cannot go back to the initial one.

Devastated, I thanked the officer and left. Furious, I contacted the producer and let her know what just happened, and nobody answered me.

A couple of weeks later, I received my check from the production and cashed it but found out the next day when the ATM receipt showed:

"We placed a hold on a check you deposited at an ATM. The full amount is not available yet." What a joke!

I contacted the production company through email again to let them know about the situation, and they fixed it. On the check, there was $500 for the participation on the show fees and $80 for my medication expenses, which was in total **FIVE HUNDRED EIGHTY DOLLARS AND 00/100**. Yes, a big shame for this production company because what about the $100 I paid for the consultation? Paid for transportation? My emotional distress? Of course, they did not care because I was a Black African. A white woman would have never been treated like that. Sad reality! This is America! But I put everything into God's hands. Only He can fight for me.

The following week, there was a film festival going on, and I grabbed my camera and microphone and went there to do what I know best: interview people. First, it was "Dance with Film" that I attended with a friend. Another week, it was the "LA Film International Film Festival" that I attended by myself, where I recorded videos and interviewed people. Lastly, I attended the "LA Shorts International Film Festival," one of the best festivals I have seen so far. Once again, I interviewed people, took pictures of them, and recorded the overall event. It was a very beautiful night with lots of memories. I covered each of those events and published them later on my social media business platform, "Africallywood."

Poupy Gaelle Nguetsop poses on the red carpet for the HollyShorts Film Festival in Hollywood

People loved it and made positive comments about it, which gave me joy and happiness. It also motivated me to keep going and work more to improve the platform and develop the business so it can be a permanent job.

A week later, I got a phone call from back home that my dad had passed away. I was shocked. I started to feel bad migraine, then fever. I stopped every activity to connect with my family back home, especially my mom, my brothers, and my sister, who was pregnant and almost ready to give birth. It was a painful moment. A moment you feel life has stopped and does not make any sense anymore. Now it was time to start thinking about preparing his funeral, which was very difficult to handle. I felt lost and alone, powerless.

I was still looking for an opportunity to make a living but also to grow my business. I was offering my service to news outlets so I could make a little bit of money from it, but nothing came of it. But I was glad that for the last school journalism project, I wrote stories for "California Humanities," which was a fellowship that awarded me $2500.00 in two payments, and also for the school magazine, which did not pay but at least the story was published.

I was so proud of my work but also of my progress. I know my writing skill is not as good as my other classmates, but I know I have that communication skill and interact with people better than them, which gives me an advantage, more importantly because I am bilingual and can report things in both languages, French and English.

It is a tough time to still find a job, and the struggle is huge. I have applied everywhere in so many places and until now have not found anything. It has been three months already, but I have hope.

While waiting, I am working on my talk show platform, "Africallywood." I run all the social media platforms myself; I plan schedules and make appointments to meet with editors and videographers myself. I have to take responsibility for everything because it is my business, and nobody really cares if you are doing great or not.

I recently applied to volunteer in the Robert F. Kennedy Presidential campaign and got accepted.

[Image Caption: Robert F. Kennedy campaign volunteer badge]

This is for me another victory and a good step for the future, especially in my journalism career. Kennedy's family is very famous in American history and politics.

While working on that project, I had a chance to meet a handsome and charming guy with whom I had a very close relationship, but unfortunately, it did not end well. He contacted me online, specifically through my Instagram page, and then we started texting each other. We had good chemistry together to the point that he invited me to meet with him the same day a little bit strange or too soon. I agreed to meet with him and later go to a dinner night so I could show him my goal for the campaign.

Chapter4: The Divorced Man

"The Divorced Man" is a romantic love story between a man I met online that ultimately turned dark. I have changed names and places to protect identities and businesses.

The story is about an alpha male living in Santa Monica, Los Angeles, who goes through a divorce and uses it as an excuse to date women, never intending to form a serious relationship. In reality, he mistreats them in many ways physically, emotionally, and intimately through manipulation and coercion. But his actions will eventually catch up with him, as one of the women he wronged takes a stand and finds a way to hold him accountable, despite his powerful reputation.

The story portrays a man whose character is manipulative, narcissistic, and abusive. He only wants his partners to obey his wishes, never the reverse. At the start, he hides his true personality in order to attract women, presenting himself as kind and attentive. Once trust is built, he gradually reveals controlling tendencies. He pressures his partners to fulfill his constant demands, whether for personal favors, compromising requests, or situations that serve his advantage. Obsessed with control, he imposes his authority in relationships as if managing a workplace, always needing the final say, otherwise rejecting the situation completely.

The story also sheds light on how dating in Hollywood can be complicated and unsafe, particularly for women of color when the man is white and wealthy.

This narrative unfolds in seven parts: how we met, when the incident happened, the investigation process and legal procedure, the verdict, and the end of the story.

How We Met

His name is Ted Waver. He is six feet tall, 43 years old, with short blond hair and green eyes. In his younger years, he was a professional tennis player, but later shifted into the entertainment industry. He is now an actor, model, and occasional event host. His career in film and commercials brought him recognition, though his brother Freddy Waver pursued tennis more seriously and is now a well-known commentator on a tennis channel. Ted, by contrast, chose another path.

Today, Ted is the president of a corporate nonprofit organization. He also trains children in tennis during his spare time. Yet alongside these activities, he enjoys chatting with women online. His preferred targets are women of all races with certain looks he favors. I describe him as a predator seeking admiration, and even his artwork reflects this mindset. For instance, one of his paintings was described as "provocative" by a woman who had once met him.

He is undeniably handsome charming, elegant, with the athletic build of a former player. A wealthy man with a magnetic smile and attractive physique, yet inwardly destructive for anyone with a sensitive heart. As the saying goes, "Everything that shines isn't always gold."

He once thrived in tennis but left after ten years, devoting himself to entertainment, where he has worked for over two decades. He has appeared in acting roles, modeling campaigns, and commercials. In addition, he invests in companies to grow his wealth. He often meets women through dating apps like Tinder and through social media, which, according to a former acquaintance, is one of his daily habits.

One day, while I was browsing Instagram, I liked a post from a presidential candidate. He apparently noticed and soon looked through my profile, liking several of my photos. One picture, from a red-carpet event I had recently attended, caught his attention. He reacted with a heart emoji, and I responded with a like and a smile. From there, we began chatting.

At that time, I had applied to volunteer for the campaign as a journalist eager to gain experience. He started asking me

45

questions, and at first, I was skeptical like many, I wondered if this was a scam, since fake profiles are common online.

It was Monday afternoon, hot and bright, around 3 to 4 p.m. on August 14, 2023. He gave me his phone number, but only after confirming I was real, since I didn't have as many followers as he did. I reassured him, and once I had his number, I quickly texted him. He wanted to be certain again that my profile was genuine. Soon after, he invited me out the same day, sending a car to pick me up.

We planned to meet at 7 p.m., giving me time to prepare. I dressed in black leggings, a long-sleeved black bodysuit, a yellow jacket, and black heels an elegant and polished look. My makeup was light and natural.

By 6:30 p.m., I messaged him that I was ready. He confirmed, sent a car, and provided the details. I waited outside and was picked up.

We met that night at 7:30 p.m. At his duplex, we switched to his car and first stopped at Office Depot to look for furniture for his office. I noticed his wedding ring and asked about it.

"I'm divorcing," he replied. "My wife returned to Russia, where she came from. You don't need to worry about that." Though a little confused, I accepted his explanation. He assured me he was free to date. For me, it felt like permission to continue spending the evening together.

Later, we went to a fine Italian restaurant in his neighborhood. We had a pleasant time there. While seated, I placed my handbag between us to keep some distance, but he encouraged me to sit closer, suggesting we should look like a real couple.

"Why are you sitting so far away? Move your handbag to the side and come closer," he said. I did as he asked, placing my bag beside me so we could speak more comfortably. He ordered ravioli with white sauce, while I chose spaghetti with tomato sauce, along with gelato for dessert and meatballs as an appetizer.

Before eating, I offered a short prayer, asking for a blessing over our time together and for protection over the meal. As a Christian, this was important to me not just for the food, but for safety and guidance in that moment.

He invited me to taste his dish, which was delicious, and I shared mine as well, which he enjoyed. He was attentive polite, considerate, and engaging. He opened doors, put his phone away, and gave me his full attention.

We spoke about hobbies, careers, and the joys they brought us. We also discussed modeling, favorite colors, and favorite ice creams. The chemistry felt natural, as though we had known each other for years.

After dinner, we returned to his house. On the way, he texted his mother, who lives with him, to let her know he was arriving with a guest.

"Do you live with your mom?" I asked.

"She lives with me. It's my house, not hers," he replied.

I was a little surprised, but it seemed he wanted to reassure me that his personal life was independent and open.

When we arrived, his mother stepped out to greet us. She was a petite woman with short blond hair, kind and welcoming. He introduced us:

"Mom, this is Poupy, my friend."

"Poupy, this is my mom, Carole."

I felt a bit shy meeting her on the very first day.

"Hi, Mrs. Carole. It's my pleasure to meet you tonight," I said politely.

"Nice to meet you too," she replied warmly before calling her two small dogs and retreating to her room.

Ted then showed me around the house. We eventually settled in his art room, which carried traces of his dog, Gaspard. He displayed his paintings with pride, and I was impressed that he had never taken formal lessons.

Two of the artworks especially caught my attention. On one wall hung a painting of two young women in water, with a large wild animal nearby, its stance threatening rather than

47

graceful.

"Isn't it beautiful?" he asked.

I thought it was more unsettling than beautiful, its imagery more ominous than inspiring.

Later, we sat on the couch to watch a movie. He asked about my favorite film, and I said *Titanic*. He suggested instead a fast-paced car-racing movie with Paul Walker and Tyrese, which we agreed on.

As the film played, we began to relax into each other's company. He grew more affectionate, kissing me gently. The moment felt cinematic, like a scene from a drama. We laughed, then kissed again. When he expressed interest in moving further physically, I gently explained that I wasn't comfortable doing so on a first date, especially given personal circumstances. He pressed a little but I firmly declined, and despite his persistence, I remained clear about my boundaries. Eventually, we ended the evening with lighter affection, finishing the film and sharing a final kiss. When midnight struck, I decided to return home. He called a car to take me back, and the evening closed on what felt like a memorable first encounter.

The following day, we texted often, exchanging playful messages and laughter. It felt almost like young love two people newly discovering each other.

That same week, on Thursday, he invited me to his place in Woodland Hills. He seemed eager to spend more time together. I declined, partly because a family friend was visiting, and partly because I still wasn't feeling my best. Instead, I suggested Saturday, when I would be more comfortable and free of obligations. He agreed without hesitation.

By Saturday, he was impatient with excitement. He kept messaging me, urging me to bring an overnight bag since his mother would be away at a concert, leaving him with the house to himself. He sent photos of himself and his dog waiting, which I found thoughtful and charming. On his way

48

home, he even offered to bring me food from a fast-food stop.

As I was getting ready, he video-called me. I answered briefly, careful not to reveal my outfit, since I wanted it to be a surprise.

"I'm sorry, sweetheart, I didn't mean to spoil your surprise. I didn't see anything," he said with a soft laugh.

Finally, when I was dressed, I let him know, and he sent a car to pick me up.

That night, I chose a small pink dress stylish and elegant paired with high heels that enhanced the look. My makeup was subtle, highlighting my features, and I styled my hair into a neat ponytail. I felt confident and ready for the evening.

Once I arrived at his duplex, he wasn't waiting outside. I texted him while I sat in the car, and after a short while, he came down. The sun was shining brightly, and the day felt full of promise. He opened the car door with a warm smile and embraced me in a gentle hug. Apologizing for the delay, he explained he had just stepped out of the shower. The faint trace of his cologne lingered in the air, comforting and inviting. Holding my hand, he led me inside.

As soon as we entered, he took my handbag and placed it on the sofa. Then, looking directly into my eyes, he came closer, cupped my face with both hands, and kissed me tenderly slow, kind, and full of emotion. The moment felt cinematic, as though we were in the middle of a romance film. There was such gentleness in the way he kissed me that I felt something shift inside; it was as though I had fallen for him right then.

After a few minutes, we went upstairs, where he suggested we paint together. I agreed, curious and excited. As he looked through the closet for something comfortable I could wear, our closeness grew stronger. He handed me a long shirt, and in that lighthearted moment, he smiled with admiration and whispered, "Waouhh." I laughed softly, and

49

before long, we were kissing again. The connection deepened, and we eventually found ourselves in the next room, beautifully decorated with a television facing the bed. There, we shared our first true moment of intimacy.

Though interrupted occasionally by his pets Gaspard and the other dogs, along with his large cat the experience felt natural and full of affection. His touch was gentle, his gaze open, and his presence disarming. It was the first time we expressed our feelings in this way, and it felt genuine, like a perfect meeting of two single people who had found each other without seeking. I hadn't gone looking for him; he had entered my life naturally, and somehow it seemed like fate.

Afterward, I stepped into the shower and noticed a few women's products, but I brushed them aside without giving them much thought. Once dressed again for our planned painting session, I joined him downstairs, wearing the oversized t-shirt he had chosen for me. He teased lightly that I could paint without clothes if I wanted, but I declined with a smile.

Back in the art room, we gathered the materials and then returned downstairs, where a tennis game played on the television. His brother Michael was among the commentators, and Ted's eyes lit up with pride as he pointed out his voice. It was clear how much he admired his brother's accomplishments.

We then began setting up the table for painting. Before we started, he offered me food from a bag he had brought earlier two chicken sandwiches, one spicy and one mild. I chose the spicy one, warmed it in the microwave, and made myself a cup of green tea to go with it. The simple meal felt comforting.

As we painted, our eyes met often, and playful energy filled the room. At one point, he smeared a touch of paint on me, and we both laughed. The moment was lighthearted and full of joy.

While rinsing the brushes, his necklace slipped off. He picked it up carefully and told me the story behind it: three pearls two small traditional beads and one larger black one.

- One of the small pearls represented his father, who had passed away.
- The second had been given to him by his mother for protection.
- The large black pearl reminded him of his best friend, who had tragically died years before.

Listening, I felt compassion for his pain. When I asked about his friend, he simply said it was a terrible moment he had come home one day to find him gone. His jaw tightened as he recounted it, his eyes clouded with grief. I hugged him, and for the first time I saw a glimpse of vulnerability beneath his confident exterior.

After a while, I lost interest in painting and drifted toward the television, watching the tennis game. It felt peaceful to sit quietly in his company. When he noticed my distraction, he joined me and suggested a break. We sat together and enjoyed the program.

Soon he asked if I wanted anything else to eat. We decided on Thai takeout fried rice and chicken for me, steak for him. Twenty minutes later, the food arrived. We sat together and ate, sharing conversation in between bites. While we ate, he texted and made a phone call. I overheard him say, "If you want to come and stay tomorrow, please feel free."

The invitation caught me off guard. He had insisted earlier that he was divorced, his wife living in Russia, but this casual remark stirred questions in my mind. Was he seeing someone else as well? The thought lingered, but I set it aside. By the time we finished dinner, it was close to 11 p.m. We went upstairs once more and put on another movie, choosing something together to end the evening in a relaxed way. The day had been full, but the connection between us seemed only to grow stronger.

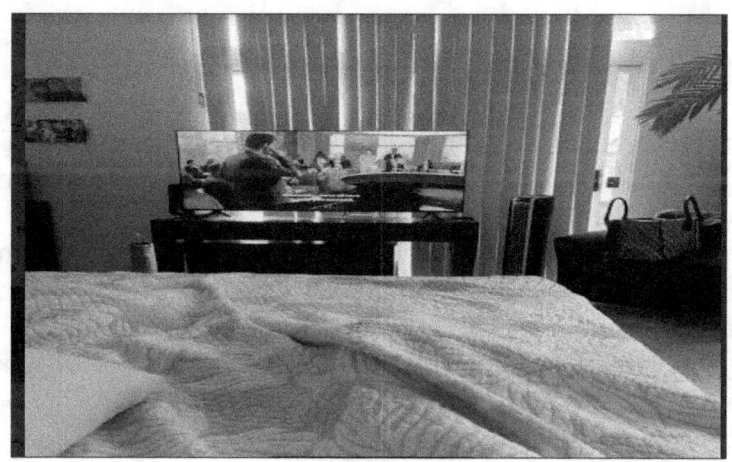

Unfortunately, as soon as the movie began, he turned toward me, and we started kissing once more. I looked at him with warmth, my eyes reflecting affection. Holding him tightly, I kissed him back, and our closeness grew into something more. That night we became intimate for the second time, even as the movie played on in the background. We laughed at how distracted we were, then eventually drifted into sleep. Around 4 a.m., I woke, took a shower, and changed into something delicate, hoping to surprise him. Returning to the bedroom, I softly woke him and whispered, "Hey, honey, look."

He gazed at me and smiled, "You look wonderful, sweetheart."

"I want you, honey," I said quietly.

But exhaustion overtook him, and he replied, "Let's rest now. Later, we will have our time."

I was disappointed but didn't want to press him further.

By morning, he woke me gently, greeted me with affection, and comforted me as I spoke about my father, whose passing still weighed heavily on me. He shared his own experience of losing his father years before, and in that moment, I felt understood. After a while, he left for a shower, then returned saying he needed to meet a business partner later in the morning. I sensed a lack of honesty, recalling how he had made a phone call the day before inviting someone else over while his mother was away at a concert.

That morning was especially hard for me grief for my father's recent passing mingled with the physical strain of a migraine. Ted held me and tried to encourage me, but my sorrow lingered.

By 9 a.m., he called for a car to take me home. It was raining heavily. He took an umbrella, walked me to the car, and opened the door for me. We exchanged a kiss, and I left.

Within twenty minutes, I was home and let him know I had arrived safely. A few hours later, I called again, telling him how much I already missed him. He seemed surprised and touched by my words.

During the following week, we stayed in touch, sharing texts about our days. But on Tuesday, the tone shifted. He asked whether I had ever been in a threesome. I answered "No." He then invited me to join one that evening, saying it would please him. I refused, telling him it wasn't something I could ever consider. He pressed again, explaining that a friend who owned a hotel was in town and wanted to meet us there. I still said no. I explained I would only even think about something like that within marriage as a private matter, not as something casual.

He grew angry, saying he expected I would do it just to please him. I reminded him that my father's funeral was taking place at that time, asking for his respect. But rather than showing compassion, he seemed fixated on his own desires, which left me hurt.

My father had believed in me, always reminding me of what I could achieve. He had been proud of my accomplishments and wanted to see my name recognized in meaningful places. To honor his memory, I could never lower myself into choices that went against everything he taught me.

The next day, Wednesday, I texted Ted just to say hello. He responded that he was on a flight to Nashville for an important campaign meeting, sending me a photo from the plane. I was surprised since he had never mentioned this trip. When I confronted him about it, he avoided explanation and instead asked me to send intimate photos. I declined, saying, "When you come back, you will see me live in front of you." He insisted, asking for new photos beyond what was already on my social media. I refused again, concerned about how such images could be misused, especially since I worked in media.

When I asked about his return, he said, "Friday."

On Thursday, while I was on a WhatsApp call with my mother, Ted attempted a video call. I didn't answer immediately but called him back after. He answered from the pool of his hotel, relaxed in the sun. We chatted pleasantly until I mentioned shopping. I told him I had just bought new heels and playfully asked, "When are we going shopping?"

"Probably not," he said.

I tried to keep the mood light, softening my tone in a playful way, but he cut the conversation short, saying he needed to prepare for the campaign event. He hung up. Later, he sent me a picture of himself with the candidate's son, which I appreciated and responded to with an emoji.

By Friday afternoon, I was eager for his return. I texted to ask if he was home yet. His reply came curtly: "Don't ever ask me for shopping again. I'm not your sugar daddy or anything like that."

Confused, I responded, "What?" I was trying to understand his sudden change of tone.

He continued: "You are not my girlfriend. I have a wife. We can just meet each other, that's it."

His words struck me like a blow. I was humiliated and speechless, sitting in silence as I processed them. Finally, I explained:

"When I mentioned shopping, it was only a way to playfully connect with you, especially since I told you on our first date that it's my favorite hobby."

But he was already angry and ended communication after that, shutting me out over what had started as a simple, playful remark.

It was heartbreaking because just a week earlier we had shared such a wonderful time together, and now, to see him grow angry over something so small, felt strange to me.

Day after day, there was silence no calls, no texts, no likes on social media. Then he posted a picture of himself among a group of people, followed by another photo with a girl who seemed very close to him. Looking more carefully, I could sense he wanted me to notice, perhaps to make me jealous.

It hurt to see those images, even though I didn't want to. Since we followed each other, every one of his posts appeared on my feed.

A few days later, the following week, he shared another photo this time with a striking woman who looked Indian or Arab, with long hair and perfect makeup. He even posted a picture of them dining together at a restaurant, just as he had done with me when we first met. But unlike me, this woman seemed to have a wider reach many followers and he openly promoted her book and encouraged people to listen to her podcast.

The sight pierced me. "Maybe I'm just jealous," I told myself. "Please, help me understand, because I can't describe this feeling."

That night, my emotions overwhelmed me. I sent him a message:

"You broke my heart! It's hard to pretend nothing happened, especially after that night we shared. I cherished it and couldn't wait for you to return, but you ruined everything over something as small as shopping? My pain is deep, and the fact that you didn't care about my feelings hurts me even more."

He replied:

"I like you, but I have a wife. I can't give you what you want. I'm sorry. You are an amazing girl."

I answered:

"But when we first met, you didn't tell me that. You said you were divorcing. That gave me the green light to open my heart again after being single and guarded for over a year."

Ted responded:

"I don't want to hurt your feelings. I don't have as much money as you may think. Whenever I do something for you, it comes from hard work. Don't assume I can provide cars or gifts every time. I don't want to feel taken advantage of."

Then he added:

"We are divorcing, but she is still around. It's complicated."

He continued:

"I never tried to hurt you. I've shown you respect since the day we met. But when you asked about shopping, it crossed a line for me. Don't try to win with me you never will. If you want me in your life, it has to be on my terms. Otherwise, goodbye."

I replied:

"We could have talked about this differently."

But he wrote back:

"No! The way you said it, and the way you reacted after I said no it wasn't right. I'm not going down the sugar daddy road. That's not who I am."

I explained:

"You were wrong when you said I acted like it was bad! We girls do that playfully all the time, even with family. If you had a sister, maybe she would explain. It's the same as the other night when I asked for more closeness and you said no I was simply trying to be lighthearted, not serious. It's called flattery. I didn't know it bothered you. Now I do."

His final reply that night was:

"Let's talk later. Maybe you can come to my hotel."

At 11:41 p.m., he texted again:

"Hey."

For three days, I didn't respond.

I began to see the pattern clearly. He was a true narcissist a manipulator. He would do something hurtful, then twist the situation to make me feel guilty for reacting.

Eventually, my curiosity drove me to research him more thoroughly. In the beginning, I had only looked at his Instagram profile, blinded by attraction. This time, I opened my laptop and searched deeper.

What I found shocked me. I discovered that a woman he had met on Tinder once accused him of assault. On December 7, 2018, a jury found him not guilty on all charges. I wasn't surprised his connections and influence were strong, enough to shield him.

Digging further, I found another report. In 2006, a woman described as his ex-girlfriend had sued him for harassment, accusing him of domestic violence and even strangling her to the point of nearly losing her life. The article was chilling.

Suddenly, everything made sense the frame on his wall, the controlling behavior, the complaints from other women. I realized the problem had never been about shopping. It was him.

I remembered the necklace he wore and how he had said it symbolized his late friend. But in one article, police identified him as the primary suspect in that very death, after his friend was found lifeless in their shared apartment.

I sat frozen, my thoughts spinning. The man I had let into my life was nothing like the image he painted of himself.

Two weeks had passed since then, and I hadn't had my period. A terrifying thought crept in: *Am I pregnant?* At 35, abortion was not an option I could consider. What if the test came back positive?

Chapter 5: The Reconnection, Then the Incidence

I wasn't pregnant. Delayed cycles can often happen when stress or worry takes hold. The Hispanic First Month Heritage celebration was approaching, and I was busy preparing for it. Ted and I had spoken about the event and its attendees, confirming that we would both be there.

The day of the campaign finally arrived, and the stress of preparing to interview the presidential candidate was heavy on my mind. I gathered all my equipment camera, microphone, tripod, and extra lenses and dressed very professionally in a pink dress paired with a black jacket. I ordered an Uber for the short ten-minute drive. The sun was shining, and the streets were clear.

Once I arrived, I followed the required protocol: checking in, receiving my name badge, and placing it on the left side of my jacket. From there, I went to the media section at the back of the ballroom. I texted him to say I had arrived. He replied, asking me to stand so he could see me. When I did, he came over, and the moment we saw each other was electric. Our excitement showed we smiled broadly, and he even pulled out his phone to take a couple of selfies of us. Then he asked:

"Would you like to stay with me at the front or remain here with the media?"

I answered that I wanted to be with him. He asked me to collect my belongings and follow him. "You'll be sitting right behind me, okay?" he added.

I smiled and said, "Okay."

We made our way to the front where the VIPs sat an area filled with notable figures. He seated me directly behind him as promised and introduced me to his friends and distinguished guests. Among them was an ambassador and councilman, attending with his long-time partner, the CEO of a major charity. There were also politicians, artists, and prominent community members.

I sat while he stood, continuing his conversations until the event began. The ceremony opened with talented dancers and a serenade that lasted about half an hour. Then came the formal announcement and entrance of the candidate for the presidency of the United States, RFK Jr. It was a moving moment, seeing him in person.

During the event, Ted couldn't hide his joy at having me there. He turned to me and whispered: "I love that pink dress on you."

I smiled warmly and replied, "Thank you."

A little later, he turned again and pinned a badge onto my blazer. Only close associates of the candidate or highly regarded guests wore it, so I understood its significance.

After the presentation, the press conference began. I rose, ready for my interview. Initially, only one line formed for those scheduled to ask questions, but later, staff created a second line. I ended up third. When my turn came, Ted moved closer, lifted his phone, and recorded me. I was nervous, but I calmed myself this was my moment.

I stepped up to the microphone, introduced myself, and asked my question:

"Mr. Kennedy, if you become the next President of the United States, what will be your roadmap toward Africa? The reason I ask is because when the last administration took office, the Vice President visited Ghana and promoted LGBTQ law, which is not part of African culture. Meanwhile, Russia trains some African militaries against local jihadism, and China is building infrastructure there. What will you do?"

His response was clear and thoughtful, which satisfied me. I returned to my seat, and Ted congratulated me for my courage.

"I'm so proud of you. You did an excellent job," he said, hugging me and showing me the clip he had recorded of my question.

Soon after, he rushed to leave, saying he had a dinner with friends. We hugged goodbye, and later that night we exchanged photos and videos from the event. I was grateful to have both my performance recorded and captured images of myself at the gathering. It felt like a privilege to be surrounded by accomplished people, sharing knowledge and expressing myself.

A few days later, around midnight, he texted to invite me over. I refused at first. He grew upset he never liked hearing the word "no." He even attempted a video call, which I ignored. Eventually, I gave in and texted back, agreeing to meet him. He sent a car to pick me up, as always.

When I arrived, it was my first time at his new residence. He had moved from the duplex where he lived with his mother and former wife. We greeted each other with a hug, both glad to reconnect. He offered me something to drink water, Coke from the fridge and even pointed out a large cake that had been saved from a recent birthday or gathering.

We stepped outside. For the first time, I saw him smoking a small cigar. We laughed, talking about the campaign event we had both attended. He showered me with compliments, telling me how proud he was, how beautiful I looked. Then, in a tone that was half-joke, half-boast, he said he wanted to visit my country, Cameroon, and take ten wives there. I forced a laugh, though his words made me uneasy. He offered me a puff of the cigar, but I declined I never smoke or drink.

When we went back inside, I helped him move a flat TV screen from his office to his bedroom so we could watch something together. He chose *Pirates*. We got into bed lightly dressed, but within minutes his hands grew demanding. He pressured me into an act I could not do. The memories of childhood abuse came rushing back, and my refusal was not a choice it was survival. I told him why. Instead of offering comfort, he grew enraged, his voice sharp and cruel, showing no compassion for my pain.

To calm him, I suggested we shower. At first, the steam and water softened the moment he washed my back, I did the same for him. But it changed quickly. His touches hardened, his insistence returned. When I resisted, his demeanor shifted from impatient to violent. His control became terrifying.

Suddenly, humiliation struck me like a slap. I cried out, asking what he was doing. His reply was crude, his tone mocking. My anger and shock erupted "No, you can't do that!" I shouted. But he sneered back, "Oh yes, I can." What followed was deliberate and degrading, meant to strip me of dignity.

Before I could escape, his hands closed around my neck, squeezing. My breath caught. He pressed harder, then slapped my face again and again, ordering me to repeat shameful words. I resisted, but his aggression escalated until I gave in, desperate for him to stop.

When he finally released me, I stumbled out of the bathroom, shaken, just wanting to leave. As I gathered my clothes, a hat he had given me earlier slipped from my hands and landed on a candle, bursting into flame. Smoke filled the room. My heart raced I grabbed my phone to call for a car, but there was no signal. Panic set in. I realized with horror I was trapped. My only option was obedience.

He unplugged the TV and we searched for the burning smell until he found the hat. His fury erupted once more, finger stabbing the air at me.

"Don't you see this is a mansion? You could have burned it down!"

Tears rolled down my cheeks. "I'm sorry baby it was just an accident."

"Don't call me baby," he barked. "I'm not your baby."

"I'm sorry, honey," I wept.

"I'm not your honey. My name is Ted," he snapped, each word like a blow.

Once the fire was out, I tried to steady myself, spraying perfume and dressing quickly. I sat on the bed, lost, confused, terrified. But he wasn't finished. His cold eyes locked on me.

"Where are you going? I'm not done yet."

He went upstairs and returned with something in his hand, his intent unmistakable. He ordered me back to bed. I refused, I begged, but he ignored every word. My pain and fear only seemed to fuel him. When I cried, he grew harsher.

At one point, he even spoke of wanting to record what he was doing. I told him no, begged him to stop. He brushed off my refusal, saying he would not show my face. My pleas made no difference his obsession with control consumed him.

When I tried to resist further, he forced me to follow him into his office. I noticed a firearm in the corner. My blood ran cold. I realized then that resistance could cost me more than dignity it could cost me my life. Terrified, I complied.

There was no intimacy, no connection only domination, only humiliation. I faked compliance to survive, because fighting back would have made it worse.

From the office, he led me into a massive conference room, cold and impersonal, with its oversized screen and long table. It was the last stop of the night. He used that space as if it were his stage, his kingdom, until finally, when his violence was spent, the ordeal ended.

Between 1 a.m. and 3 a.m., the nightmare stretched on. I was terrified, mortified, and powerless, while he seemed energized by his own cruelty. I was in pain, yet he never cared. Worse still, he filmed himself throughout without my consent, almost boasting about it. The ordeal felt endless, like hours trapped in a cage I couldn't escape.

When it was finally over, I went to the shower, desperate to wash away the night. He tried to act as though nothing had happened, inviting me to watch a movie and sleep. I couldn't close my eyes. My body was frozen, my spirit shaking. I asked him to send me home because I needed to be on set at 6 a.m. At first, he refused he wanted me to stay until morning. But I pressed, insisting I had to leave. Reluctantly, he called a car.

Just minutes after leaving his mansion, my phone buzzed. He had sent me a photo an image of me taken in the most humiliating moment of the night accompanied by the words: *"So so hot."*

The sight of it choked me. I had told him not to record me, not to take any pictures. But he had done it anyway, proud of breaking my boundaries. My instinct was to respond with outrage, but fear overruled. I wrote back simply: *"I hope you enjoyed it."* That wasn't how I truly felt it was survival. I couldn't risk angering him further. What if he called the driver? What if he had me brought back? I stayed silent, appeasing him until I was safely home.

Once inside, I locked myself in the bathroom, sank to the floor, and sobbed until my face was swollen. I even took a picture of myself crying, proof of the wreckage he had caused.

The next day, I tried to confront him. I called first, but he didn't answer. Later, he texted from Malibu, saying he was at another campaign event with RFK Jr. I pressed him: "I didn't appreciate your behavior last night. What was that? You were rude and aggressive."

He deflected coldly:

"I just don't like women spreading their bad perfume on my bed."

I insisted, "If you didn't like my perfume, why didn't you just wait and buy me another next time, or say it kindly?"

Finally, he muttered: "I'm sorry I hurt you. I promise to be nice next time."

But I had already decided there would not be a next time. When I told him that, he blocked me. Once again, I was punished simply for confronting him.

For two or three weeks, we had no contact. That same day, though, I began writing everything down from the first moment we met until that night. It became my way to heal, to take back some control. At one point, I even went to the police, ready to report what had happened. But fear stopped me. What if they didn't believe me? What if they accused me of chasing his money or his fame? I went back home and continued writing, tears streaming, reminding myself that no one deserves such treatment.

I was in love, and that blinded me. But when I read the stories of his exes, I saw the pattern. I wasn't imagining it he had done the same to others before me. That gave me resolve. If I couldn't report him yet, I would gather evidence proof that one day could bring justice.

After weeks of silence, he unblocked me. At 4 a.m., a message appeared: *"I'm giving you a second chance."*

When I woke at 6 a.m. and saw it, I tapped "like." He immediately replied: *"Please come over."*

Fear knotted in my stomach. The thought of returning horrified me, yet another thought pushed me forward this might be my only chance to collect more evidence. My choice was survival. My decision was strategy.

On my way, I took precautions. I asked him to share the ride link. I saved a screenshot of the pickup and drop-off destinations, keeping his address for safety. When I arrived, the first thing I asked for was the Wi-Fi password, pretending it was to message my mother. He wrote it on a small slip of paper kept on top of a newspaper in his conference room. I snapped a photo discreetly another piece of proof.

Then he drew me toward his bedroom. It was 7:40 a.m. I didn't want to be there, but I went along, knowing my safety depended on appearing compliant.

Only minutes into it, his business partner and closest friend, Zack, arrived. Ted immediately pulled on beige pants, a white shirt, and a hat for the campaign. He told me to stay

64

put, locked the door, and warned me not to make a sound. He didn't want his friend to know I was there. And then he left, leaving me in silence, trapped once again.

It felt as though God had been listening to my prayers at that moment. I stood and reached for my handbag, which I had left on a chair in the corner. As I lifted it, the bottle of water inside slipped out and hit the floor. The noise echoed.

He rushed back, opened the door, and glared at me.

"I told you not to make noise, right? What is happening here?"

My heart pounded. In the softest voice I could manage, I whispered, "Sorry, it was just my water bottle." He stared for a moment, then left again.

Shaking, I saw his wallet at the corner of the bed. Moving carefully, I opened it, slid out his ID card, and took a picture before emailing it to myself. I did the same with his business card. Then I placed everything back exactly as I had found it. I noticed his credit and debit cards, but I didn't touch them. Stealing had never been my intention I wanted truth, not theft.

I also snapped a photo of myself in his bedroom to prove I had been there something undeniable if I ever needed to show it. When I finished, I emailed all the files to myself and deleted them from my gallery in case he ever searched my phone.

When he returned, I grabbed the robe I had brought from home and told him I wanted coffee. I didn't want to stay in that room with him. He let me leave, and I went to his office, where the coffee machine was. I made two cups and turned on the TV, distracting myself with a game show. Fifteen minutes later, he appeared, pacing with his phone pressed to his ear.

I offered him coffee. He accepted but barely noticed me. He was frustrated after a video meeting with his campaign partners, angry at one participant's disrespect. He called

Zack, his business partner, to complain, stalking the office like a man possessed.

Afterward, we stepped outside for air. He lit another cigar, watching me while I sat in silence. His dogs bounded toward him, and he bent down to kiss them on the mouth. Then he leaned toward me to do the same, but I turned away. I wasn't comfortable, and he didn't like that refusal.

Lunch was ordered. While waiting, he went upstairs, and I stayed behind in the office. I returned to my game show, but when he came back, he snatched the remote, changed the channel to tennis, and said sharply, "Who watches that kind of program nowadays!" His tone was dismissive, belittling. The air between us grew colder.

When the food arrived, he unpacked a salad for me and noodle soup for himself. I had no appetite and couldn't eat. He received a call from a woman he described as one of the house owners. She was on her way to deliver campaign materials. He turned to me and said bluntly that I had to leave. They couldn't see me there.

Once again, it felt like God had given me an exit. I rushed to the bedroom, changed, and packed my bag. I didn't touch the food. I had no appetite, no desire to stay a moment longer.

On my way out, he held my handbag. I took the chance to snap another selfie in the house this time with him in the frame, proof that I had been there. Piece by piece, I was gathering evidence. But still, I couldn't speak out.

Silence followed. Days passed with no words exchanged between us. Then one day, he invited me again. I refused. Not only because of what he had done to me, but because I finally saw him clearly manipulative, narcissistic, insensitive. He had dragged me into his world yet never offered even the smallest help, not for my bills or for my work. Wealth did not mean generosity, and he was proof of it.

The next day, he invited me again. Again, I said no. This time, his temper broke.

"Come here now!" he demanded.

"No," I replied.

He laughed cruelly. "Hahaha, then you will never see me again. You won't win against me. Sorry."

"Then bye, Ted," I said firmly.

"Okay, bye," he shot back, but moments later insisted again.

Trying to change the subject, I said, "My birthday is coming, November 26th."

His response was ice cold:

"Look, you will never win against me. I invited you two days in a row, and you said no. So I will say no when you ask me for something. Do you want me to forget you and block you? Because I can. Or you can be smart, come over here, and see me. Your choice. Don't ever ask me for money again.

You think saying no gives you power? Listen you will never win against me."

I confronted him. I told him he always demanded I come over, as if I had no life of my own. That he was egotistical, always twisting things to put the blame on me.

When he barked again, "I want you to come here right now," the tone was sharp, commanding, as if he owned me. I said no.

That was the end. I blocked him on Instagram, deleted his number, and chose silence.

Chapter 6: The Infection, The Cease and Desist Notice & Investigation

A couple of weeks later, my body began sending warning signs. Each time I went to the restroom, there was a discharge with a strong, fishy smell, and the itching grew unbearable. The discomfort haunted me. Desperate, I went to Walgreens and bought Monistat, hoping the over-the-counter medicine would help. I used it faithfully for three days, following the instructions carefully, but nothing changed.

As days passed, I realized the problem was far more serious. Reluctantly, I went to the hospital. I checked in, my heart pounding with shame, then sat in the waiting room until a nurse finally called my name. She struggled to pronounce it, but I raised my hand and whispered, "Here."

She led me inside, measured my weight, pulse, and blood pressure, then handed me a small cup for a urine test. When the pregnancy test came back negative, I should have felt relief but the fear of something worse loomed over me. The nurse gave me a gown and directed me to a private room. I sat on the bed, heavy with sadness, waiting for the doctor.

When he entered, I couldn't bring myself to explain what had happened with Ted. Shame pinned my tongue. He examined me gently, his voice calm and reassuring, telling me I had nothing to be embarrassed about. His kindness was a contrast to everything I had endured, but I still left feeling hollow. He promised to email the results once the tests were complete.

The next day was Thanksgiving silence. The day after, I received the email: a bacterial infection, an STD. My stomach sank. Along with the diagnosis came a prescription for a cream. I held the message in my hands, my heart racing with humiliation and anger.

I tried to tell him. I texted him, attaching the doctor's note. No response. I forgot he had blocked me, and I had blocked him. I tried again through Instagram, then by email. Still nothing. My words dissolved into silence.

I wrestled with myself. Who could I tell? His mother? No I had met her only once, and how could I possibly tell her something so personal about her son? His brother? No we had never met, and he would only be confused.

Finally, I turned to his best friend and business partner, Zack, the man he had introduced me to during the Hispanic Heritage Month celebration. I introduced myself again, explained why I was reaching out, and pleaded with him to speak to Ted. I told him I was exhausted, broken, and asked for $200,000 compensation for medical costs, emotional distress, and everything I had endured. I wanted to resolve it quietly, respectfully, even though I knew such a request would wound his pride. If not, I told him, I would have no choice but to file a lawsuit and make everything public.

But instead of a response from him, I received one from his lawyer. Within 24 hours, a cease-and-desist letter landed in my inbox. It was intimidation in black and white. The letter accused me of spreading lies, demanded that I write a statement recanting my words, and threatened legal action if I didn't comply within ten days.

I never replied. I never signed anything. That letter only steeled my resolve.

Two years have passed since then, and I am still determined to fight for my life and my rights. From that moment on, I began speaking out in the safest ways I could.

I turned to someone I trusted deeply my journalism professor, Yolanda Ross, a woman I respected and loved like a second mother.

That day, I took the metro to school, tears threatening to fall the whole way. As soon as I arrived, I called her while crying:

"Professor, professor, are you on campus?"

Her voice was soft but alarmed. "What's going on?"

"Where are you?" I asked, choking on the words.

"I'm at the front door," she said. Then after a pause: "Actually, I'm heading into a meeting at the Student Union." I hung up and walked quickly through the sun, unprotected, not caring if I burned. My fear and shame were heavier than the heat.

At the building, I texted her again, letting her know I was downstairs. She told me to come up. On the second floor, she slipped out of her meeting to see me.

When she saw me shaking, her eyes softened. She stayed with me, urging me gently until, at last, I began to speak the words I had been holding in for too long.

It took me a few minutes before I could share everything with her. Piece by piece, the story came out, and without hesitation, she urged me: *"You need to go to the police station and report this right away."*

I was embarrassed to reveal so much of my personal life, but she had always been someone I confided in. I had told her about every red carpet I attended, my volunteer work on RFK Jr.'s campaign, my father's passing, and the progress of my media platform. Sharing this was painful, but not impossible. We hugged tightly before I left.

The next morning, I woke early, showered, dressed, and gathered the strength to leave for the police station. On the way, I stopped to print photos and text messages from my phone as evidence. It took almost two hours, but I knew I had to prepare myself fully.

My first stop was the LAPD headquarters in Downtown Los Angeles the "heart of the LAPD." To my disappointment, the facility was only for employees, not open to the public. The officer at the desk redirected me to another location. So I boarded a bus and rode 35 minutes to get there.

At the station, a male officer greeted me with kindness. He asked me why I had come, and I told him everything. Then he asked me to wait until two female officers arrived so I could give my statement in a way that felt safe and respectful.

After about 20 minutes, the two officers came. They led me to a private room, where I finally told the story for the record. For nearly two hours, they listened, asked questions, and carefully documented everything. When it was over, they handed me a copy of my police report. For the first time in weeks, I felt the air return to my lungs. I thanked them and stepped back out into the cold, dark night.

On the bus ride home, I thought about what I had done. By the time I got back, I was drained. I showered, skipped dinner, and went straight to bed. I wasn't hungry I was simply relieved.

The next morning, I woke up lighter. I had finally spoken out, not just to doctors but to law enforcement. I was no longer holding everything inside. But the fight wasn't over. I needed legal representation to respond to the cease-and-desist letter he had sent me.

I started making phone calls. I reached out to *Peace of Violence*, a nonprofit. They listened, wrote down my story, but offered no legal help. I called several other organizations, only to meet the same dead end. It was crushing being left without support in such a critical moment.

My professor reached out again. She advised me to speak to Joseph "JoJo" Exoneski, the school's supervisor and counselor. I agreed. My first session with him was calming twenty to thirty minutes of gentle conversation. He listened, took notes, gave advice, and offered recommendations. For the first time, I felt seen in a safe space.

The following Tuesday, I received a private phone call. Not a counselor, not an officer but a detective. Her name was Milla H. We spoke for nearly two hours, with a short break in between. She asked me to recount everything from the very beginning when I met him on Instagram to the last day I spoke to him, November 19, 2023.

At the end of our conversation, she explained: "I'm collecting all of this and will send it to the district attorney's office. They will decide whether charges will be filed."

Her words gave me hope, though she also reminded me that because of the holiday season, everything would pause until after Christmas.

For the first time, I felt that justice was possible.

Chapter 7: In Pursuit of an Ally: Navigating the Legal Labyrinth

When we returned from the Christmas holidays, the days felt quiet and still, as if the whole world had pressed pause. I waited, expecting at any moment to hear from the detective. One week passed. Nothing. Then another week slipped by. Still silence. Each day that ticked by without a call made the weight on my chest heavier. I told myself to be patient, but deep inside, the waiting was eating me alive.

During that time, I had a scheduled school counseling meeting over video. The purpose was simple: to evaluate whether I should take more classes in order to transfer to a university, or whether I should completely change my career path. But the meeting turned into something else. As soon as the conversation began, emotions flooded me. I couldn't stop myself. Everything I had endured came crashing down all at once the abuse, the lies, the silence, the recent passing of my father. I felt weak, broken, and uncertain about my future.

The counselor on the other side of the screen noticed immediately. My voice cracked, my tears blurred the camera. The weight of it all spilled out, and the host paused the academic conversation to focus on my wellbeing. Gently but firmly, they told me that without addressing my mental health, I would not be able to move forward with school, career, or any plans. I needed help immediately. The meeting ended with me sobbing uncontrollably, my body shaking from the release of emotions I had been bottling inside for too long.

Minutes later, I received a call from a therapist. It wasn't the same counselor I had seen before; this time, it was a woman. She spoke kindly, with patience, allowing me space to cry while she listened. Her voice was soothing, steady, like a rope pulling me out of quicksand. She scheduled a fast-track appointment for me within three days.

The first meeting was over Zoom. We spent an hour together, and she allowed me to walk through everything from the beginning. She made notes, nodding gently, interjecting with suggestions and recommendations that gave me some clarity. For the first time in a long while, I felt I was being heard without judgment.

Four days later, on Friday at 1 p.m., we met again, this time in person. Sitting face to face was different it was heavier but also more healing. Her name was Sadia. She was an intern, young, but she carried herself with calm confidence and treated me with the utmost respect. She checked in constantly, making sure I felt safe, making sure the session was constructive. Another hour passed, and when it was over, I left feeling lighter. She helped me see that healing was not only possible but already beginning.

The following Friday, at the same hour, we met once more. This time, I walked in with my head slightly higher. Sadia's presence gave me courage. She asked about my week, listened intently, and guided me through strategies to focus on the positive. That session ended with me feeling a bolt of energy and gratitude. For the first time in months, I had something to hold on to hope.

But even with therapy, the silence from the justice system was deafening. Two months had already passed since I had filed the police report and spoken with the detective. Still, no feedback, no update, no sign that my case mattered. To fill that void, I began reaching out to lawyers, determined to find representation. What followed was a cascade of rejections.

The first law firm responded politely but coldly:

"Hi Poupy Gaelle, we're sorry we couldn't help with this case. Below, you can find the California Bar Association number, as they oversee all state attorneys and might be able to assist in finding other legal representation. We wish you the best of luck with your current situation."

Reading those words felt like a door slammed in my face.

Another firm took longer, reviewing the details I had sent. Their answer arrived after internal discussions, but the message was the same:

"We have completed our review of the initial information you provided us regarding your potential lawsuit, and we have discussed the matter with other members of the firm. While we appreciate the confidence you have expressed in our firm, for various reasons we have determined that we are unable to represent you in this matter. In declining your case, we are not expressing an opinion about the merits of your potential lawsuit, and our decision should not be interpreted as an adverse opinion about the strength of your claim or your chance of success if you pursue the matter."

The words stung not because they doubted me, but because they refused to stand with me.

Then came a third response, this time from a high-profile law firm. The language was polished, almost elegant, but the meaning was the same rejection.

"Dear Ms. Poupy Nguetsop, thank you for contacting our Law firm, in regard to legal matters and for allowing our office the opportunity to review your potential case. Unfortunately, it is with the utmost regret that I must inform you, upon further review of the information you provided, our office has made the difficult decision not to take on your case, and we have closed our files. Thus, our office will not be pursuing any further action on your behalf. This does not necessarily mean that you do not have a case; therefore, we recommend you seek other legal representation immediately."

By the time I finished reading, my chest ached. I felt invisible, rejected not because of the facts of my case, but because of who I was. My race. My status. My background. I felt racially profiled, judged, and silenced. It was as if no one wanted to believe me, no one wanted to help me, and the world had decided my suffering was unworthy of attention. The pain of rejection piled onto the pain of injustice.

People will always have their own opinions. They may dismiss me, criticize me, or doubt me. But I know one truth: at the end of the day, I am the one living this pain. I am the one carrying the scars.

Five months later, another blow struck. On April 21, 2024, I lost my job. The reason was not performance but discrimination, mistreatment, and unfair treatment from my manager. That night is burned into my memory.

Additionally, to the stress I was experiencing already pushing me to a forced resignation.

It was a Sunday evening, between 10:15 and 10:30 p.m., during my shift as a cashier at a restaurant on Hollywood Blvd and Highland. The manager suddenly grew furious because I had given two customers extra dressings with their meal.

"Why did you give them those dressings?" he barked.

"Why not?" I answered honestly.

He didn't like my response. His tone rose, sharp and aggressive. He accused me of doing things I shouldn't, even though I reminded him that other managers had no issue with my service. In fact, I often received good reviews from customers. But he wasn't listening. His anger only grew.

He ordered me to leave the restaurant immediately. I refused, calmly explaining that my shift wasn't over until 11 p.m., and I would clock out then. He refused to accept that, chasing me through the restaurant, demanding that I leave.

He escalated further by calling another coworker from upstairs to help him push me out, treating me as though I were a thief, not an employee. I remained calm, continuing my work, unwilling to be dragged into chaos.

Not satisfied, he called the main manager, Walker, who was already home. I called too, hoping for fairness, but Walker didn't answer my call. Instead, he texted me: "Clock out and obey the other manager. He is your supervisor." His words stung no support, no fairness, just dismissal.

So I clocked out and left. But that night left scars. I received fewer tips than the white cashiers, Aiden and Jess. My paycheck showed only 18 hours instead of the 20 I had worked. The discrimination was clear, and the humiliation unbearable.

The stress pushed me to resign. I could not continue working in an environment that degraded me.

So I took action. I filed a small claim against the manager and the company. In my statement, I wrote:

"Today, I am taking action by filing a small claim against my manager from the restaurant located in Hollywood Blvd Highland for discrimination, mistreatment, and extreme verbal abuse during my duty time at that place.

The incident occurred on Sunday night April 21, 2024, at around 10:15 p.m. to 10:30 p.m.

This manager appeared extremely and verbally aggressive toward me because I gave away two dressings (ranch sauces) to customers during their dinner. He asked why I gave them those dressings. I replied, 'Why not?' He told me I shouldn't, and I reminded him that when he isn't there, I work with other managers and everything is fine, often receiving good reviews.

He became furious, forced me to engage with him, and when I walked away, he followed me. He demanded that I leave immediately. I explained I was scheduled until closing and would leave at 11 p.m., but he refused. He even brought another coworker to pressure me out as though I were an outsider.

Later, he called the main manager, Walker, who told me by text to obey. I respected his words, clocked out, and left.

As a consequence, I received fewer tips and less direct deposit than I was owed. I was paid for only 18 hours instead of 20. The situation caused me emotional distress and financial loss, forcing me to resign. I invite the judge to review the evidence and help me get the justice I deserve."

After careful consideration, the employment lawyer who initially reviewed my case admitted there was definitely a claim in what had happened with my manager. His words gave me a brief flicker of hope. But just as quickly, that hope was snatched away. He said that unfortunately his firm could not assist me directly. Instead, he referred me to another law firm, assuring me they would handle the situation.

I clung to that referral as if it were a lifeline. The second law firm reached out. We went over my small claim in detail, reviewing the evidence, talking through the events that had led me to resign. For hours, I poured out my side of the story again. When the call ended, I waited nervously, believing this might finally be the beginning of justice.

But only a couple of hours later, an email landed in my inbox. It was another rejection. They wrote that they would not be able to assist me. My heart sank. I felt abandoned again, and this time even more bitter because the fault clearly came from my manager, not me.

As if to twist the knife, my final paycheck arrived two weeks later instead of within 72 hours, as required by state law. Even the most basic right to be paid what I had earned was delayed.

In the meantime, I filed for Unemployment Insurance, hoping I could receive benefits while looking for another job and while waiting for my claim to be processed. Once again, I was denied. The letter said I was "disqualified" because I had resigned voluntarily instead of being fired. My stomach dropped. That money would have been my only source of income. Losing it felt like being pushed into a dark hole without a rope.

I cried until my body ached. I contacted my school's foundation, begging for help, but they told me they had "dispensed all their funds." Their words hit me like a door slammed shut. I felt utterly alone.

I reached out to friends, both here and abroad, hoping for some kindness, some support. Phones went unanswered. Excuses piled up. Promises evaporated. My rent was already overdue by a week, and panic pressed in on me.

In the end, it was my family who saved me. My sister, who had just given birth to her fifth child, sent me what little she could. My brother back home in Cameroon also sent me something, enough to keep in my pocket and help me cover my rent. With their help, I not only paid that month's rent but managed to save a little for the next month, sparing me from having to beg again.

It was then I realized the truth: in moments of crisis, you see the real faces around you. Many people I had trusted disappeared, their phones silent. The hypocrisy of certain people in the industry was glaring. I had covered countless stories as a journalist stories about people of every race, every background, every walk of life. But when it was my turn to need coverage, to ask my fellow journalists to share my truth, none of them came forward. No one reached out. Not one.

The betrayal stung. I told myself maybe it was "fair," maybe people were busy. But inside, I was bitter. I had given my voice to amplify others, but when I needed mine to be heard, silence swallowed me whole.

The emptiness grew. I lost the taste of life, the excitement of doing the things I once loved. Insomnia took over my nights. Depression sat heavy on my chest. I applied to the California Victim Compensation Board, desperate for some form of relief, but the process was slow 90 to 100 days before even knowing if I would be approved. Three long months of waiting, with no guarantees.

By then, seven months had already passed since I had reported everything to the police. The investigation was still incomplete. The district attorney had still not decided whether to prosecute. Each day of waiting made my anxiety worse, my pain deeper.

To escape the weight of it all, I went to meet a friend staying at a hostel. She was visiting from France, and for a moment, it felt good to talk about something other than my own suffering. In our conversations, I realized I wasn't the only one hurting. Other people carried heartbreak too. That night, I heard the story of Yu Li, and it left me speechless.

Yu Li and I met in Koreatown, Los Angeles, at the hostel where she was staying. She was 31 years old, originally from Japan, but living in England for work. She told me she had come to the U.S. to breathe fresh air, to see new places, and to take distance from her boyfriend and his ex-girlfriend. Her English was limited but clear enough to understand. She was 5'4", calm, and respectful. As she opened up, I could hear the pain in her voice. She explained that she had been in a relationship with a European man from England for three years. Despite all that time, they had no plans for the future. She wanted a family, children, stability. But he procrastinated every conversation, refusing to commit.

Worse, his ex-girlfriend remained in his life. Not only did they share a business together, but whenever the ex came around, Yu Li had to leave his house. She described the humiliation being pushed aside, treated as if she were temporary. Her boyfriend explained that he had spent thirteen years with his ex, never married, never had children, but kept the business alive with her. For Yu Li, it was unbearable. She admitted she was furious and heartbroken.

She confessed that her dream was to return to Japan, find a man who truly wanted marriage and children, and start fresh. She said her mother also urged her to come back, reminding her that no one knows you better than your own family.

Yu Li was a barista in England, proud of her work, but her eyes revealed exhaustion. She said she had already traveled to Las Vegas, Dallas, New York, and now Los Angeles, trying to find peace through new places, new people, new cultures. But the hurt followed her. Her boyfriend had sent

80

her text after text during her travels, but she didn't respond. She wanted to call it quits.

I listened, and then I told her: "Follow your heart. Listen to your mother. She sees what you cannot."

She looked at me with gratitude. She appreciated the advice, the simple reminder that sometimes the answer is to leave behind what is hurting you.

As she finished, another roommate stepped forward to share her own story. That night at the hostel, surrounded by strangers, I realized that pain has many faces and many voices. And though each story is different, the need for healing is the same.

My name is Radjina. I am from Iran, and here is my story.

I am an architect, and for many years, I believed I was blessed beyond measure. I had married a kind, handsome man, also an architect, and together we built what I thought was a solid, beautiful life. We decided to open a business, pooling our talents into projects that not only paid the bills but also supported the lifestyle we dreamed of. Everything seemed perfect. We bought a house in Beverly Hills, elegant and spacious, the kind of place I once thought only existed in dreams. We opened a joint business account, and the money from our projects flowed into it.

I never cared much about the finances; I trusted him completely. He handled the paperwork, the accounts, the complicated side of things, while I poured myself into additional work and the creative aspects of our projects. For five years, our marriage looked perfect on the outside but slowly, cracks began to appear. He spent more time away, working late without explanation, guarding his phone, becoming distant in ways I couldn't name but could feel in my bones.

One day, I discovered the truth. He had been hiding debts $70,000 worth of bills paid without my knowledge. When I confronted him, he brushed it off. But things grew worse, and soon after, I found out the unthinkable: he had a mistress. My heart broke. I confronted him again, but instead of remorse or reconciliation, he coldly asked for a divorce.

I couldn't process it. My mother, seeing my despair, invited me to return home to Iran for a short stay, hoping I could heal. I went, planning to stay one month, but left after two weeks, believing I was strong enough to face my reality. I was wrong.

When I landed back in Los Angeles, I ordered an Uber and headed to my home in Beverly Hills. But when I inserted my key into the lock, it didn't turn. I tried again, then tried the back door. Nothing. Confused, I called my husband. His voice was calm, almost smug, when he told me: "Yes, I changed all the locks."

I stood frozen on the doorstep of the house I thought was mine. I ran to the garage to get my car, but it wasn't there. Later, I would learn he had taken both cars and parked them at the airport before leaving with his mistress.

I was devastated, stripped of everything in an instant. With nowhere to go, I dragged my suitcase to the nearest hostel and spent my first night there, surrounded by strangers in a room with bunk beds. From Beverly Hills to a shared dormitory it felt like a cruel joke.

The next day, depressed and broken, I went to the hospital. At the front desk, they asked for my insurance card. I handed it over, but the nurse told me it was no longer valid. My husband had cut me off, removing me from the plan linked to our business. That humiliation stung more than the rejection itself.

The doctor was kind, but there was little he could do beyond listen. I left feeling empty, my life reduced to fragments: no house, no car, no money, no health insurance, and no marriage. Back at the hostel, every night became torture. The noise of people slamming doors, cooking at odd hours, burning food that triggered the fire alarms sleep was impossible. I lost weight rapidly, my appetite gone.

I had a lawyer working on the divorce, waiting for the judge's decision so I could recover some of my belongings, but the waiting felt endless. My friends urged me to leave Los Angeles, some suggesting Colorado. I couldn't decide. I walked the streets, hating life, blaming everyone around me, and blaming myself.

I was also mourning what I never had. I had dreamed of becoming a mother, of carrying a baby, raising a family. That dream was gone now. My brothers, both married, supported me as best as they could, but I longed for the comfort of a sister's presence. I was the only daughter in my family, and the loneliness felt unbearable.

After two weeks at the hostel, my soul could no longer bear the confinement. A close friend in Chicago invited me to share her apartment. Her invitation came like a Christmas gift, not just for me, but for her children who welcomed me into their home. Grateful beyond words, I left Los Angeles.

As I packed, I told myself: this is the beginning of a new life. One thing is certain I will never marry again. I want to heal, rebuild myself, and reclaim my independence.

Hearing Radjina's story shook me. I realized pain wears many faces, and betrayal can strip people of everything they hold dear. From Beverly Hills to a hostel bunk bed, her story was proof of how fragile stability can be.

I thought of my own struggles, and I couldn't help but connect her suffering with mine. These situations, as devastating as they are, create ripple effects in our society mental health crises, financial collapse, broken dreams that are hard to heal and cost more than people imagine. Life, I realized, is a process. We experience love, hurt, betrayal, and sometimes unbearable grief, but we also experience joy, healing, and rebirth.

Yesterday, as if to remind me that life moves in circles, I was contacted by a successful journalist and producer I had met a year ago on the red carpet. Reconnecting with her lifted my spirit. She asked me how things were, and the only word I could find was, "slow."

She told me about her current work. She had been sent to Los Angeles by a UK network company to develop a program for their audience. On top of that, she was launching her own luxury clothing line. She wanted me to assist her managing things she couldn't handle due to her schedule and also to coordinate talent for the new show she was creating. I was thrilled. It felt like the universe was finally opening a door for me.

On Saturday afternoon, we met at her building at 3:30 p.m. She gave me a tour of the luxury space. It was breathtaking: a gym, a social media lounge, meeting rooms, co-working spaces for tenants, a barbecue area, and the crown jewel a pool with private seating areas for visitors. The view from the building was magnificent, the kind of view that makes you believe life can still be beautiful.

After the tour, we sat down and started working. For the first time in months, I felt hope return.

We placed special emphasis on every detail of the upcoming event: the location, the catering, the beverages, the music, the decoration, the logo, the mannequins, the public relations strategy, and everything else necessary to bring it to life. My responsibility was to handle the next steps. That meant going downtown on Monday to search for designers, both for the logo and for the banner of the event. We also agreed to meet again the following day to visit potential venues together. But on Sunday morning, she texted to cancel. It was fine with me.

So, on Monday, as planned, I went downtown Broadway on my own. I took the train and spent almost four and a half hours moving from place to place, speaking with designers, collecting information, taking notes, gathering business cards, and making contacts. When I was finished, I returned home, organized everything into a detailed report, and emailed it to her with pictures of locations and the cards I had collected. She never replied to the email itself, but later texted me saying she would look at it when she had time.

The following day, Tuesday, she texted again, this time asking how much I had spent on transportation. I responded that I intended to send her a full invoice at the end of the week since there was still much to do, unless she preferred to pay me weekly at a set rate $750 or $1000. She rejected the idea, explaining that she couldn't agree to a fixed weekly pay because she didn't yet know how many tasks she would assign me. Instead, she offered, "I will pay you $15 per hour. Is that okay for you?"

I was shocked. I replied immediately: "$15 is too low not even minimum wage. Restaurant employees make $20 per hour, and you want to pay me less? No, I can't."

This is the sad reality many of us face after graduation. We believe our degrees and professional experience will bring us opportunities with fair compensation, but the opposite often happens. Imagine me with a diploma and four years of solid experience in the field being offered $15 an hour for the role of a personal assistant to a well-connected professional? It felt like an insult. Yes, I've humbled myself in the past by taking smaller jobs, but being directly contacted for this role should have meant she recognized my work ethic and qualifications. At that moment, I promised myself never to let anyone devalue me again. If someone cannot afford my time and expertise, then they should pass.

I reminded myself of stories I had heard about certain employers exploiting workers. I recalled how one Indian diplomat in the U.S. made headlines years ago when her maid reported her for underpayment and mistreatment. That scandal went viral, damaging reputations in the international community. Such examples show how common unfair treatment is.

A few minutes later, she texted again, changing her offer: "I'll pay you $20 per hour, which is the standard for personal assistants." Relieved, I agreed, and we closed the deal. But reality set in quickly. For the entire week, she never followed up with tasks or meetings. She avoided assigning work, making it impossible for me to accumulate hours. By the end of the week, I had only logged four and a half hours, totaling a mere $90. It was humiliating.

The next week, on Tuesday, she contacted me again. She apologized for not replying earlier, saying she had been overwhelmed with other projects. She asked me to send my invoice and even provided her own template. When I opened the document, I saw entries for others working under her social media managers at $15 an hour, two hours of work. I was mortified. Still, I submitted my invoice. By Friday, two weeks after I had completed the work, I still hadn't been paid the $90. I was speechless and disheartened, especially since I had turned down another opportunity just to work with her.

The irony is bitter. I run my own TV show, but because of financial hardship, I sometimes accept jobs assisting others to make ends meet. Living in Los Angeles is expensive, especially with rising inflation. Employers should respect both the time and value of those they hire. I enjoy working it gives me purpose, it makes me feel productive, and it allows me to contribute to society. But when someone reaches out to me for help and then refuses to respect my time or value my effort, it feels like betrayal. Many immigrants experience this same injustice: low wages, empty promises, and poor treatment. And I can't help but wonder would she have treated a white assistant this way? Probably not. What I read in articles about inequity, I was now living firsthand.

By Monday, January 24, 2024, two weeks had passed with no response to my email about the work I had completed. Tired of waiting, I decided to send her a direct text:

"Good morning, I hope you had a wonderful weekend. Well, the reason I'm contacting you today is because after careful reflection and analysis I will no longer be your personal assistant due to the lack of work and communication. I started your project with passion, joy, and excitement, but you dropped it off. I like being productive, and this is not working for me. Please note I still haven't received payment from the invoice. It would be helpful if you could settle it. I hope you will find another assistant who will put as much energy and love into your project as I did. Have a wonderful day. Sincerely, Poupy."

She replied quickly: "Good morning, Poupy, my weekend was working all weekend. I'm so sorry for my lack of communication. I've literally had filming every day this week and haven't had time to attend to my fashion line. I really appreciate your passion and hard work, and I don't want to lose you. I will call you this morning, and after we chat, I'll 100 percent pay you today. I'll call between 10:30 a.m. and 11:15 a.m. Thanks."

Minutes later, another message followed: "Sorry, I'll call you at 12 p.m."

She eventually called at 12:15. During the call, we went over everything I had done two weeks earlier something that should have been acknowledged long before. Finally, she sent me $90 through Zelle. Imagine telling people you work as a personal assistant, but only getting paid $90 for two weeks of effort. Who does that? And in Los Angeles, of all places?

We agreed to move forward, scheduling a meeting the next morning to review a sample jacket for her fashion line so that the printer could determine where to place her logo. But once again, disappointment followed. At 9 a.m., no text. By 9:30, still nothing. By 9:50, I messaged her to ask when she planned to pick me up. Her response: "Good morning, Poupy. I actually got pulled into work this morning. I don't think I can come today. Let's shoot for tomorrow."

She knew we had plans, yet never bothered to notify me beforehand. I had been ready since 8 a.m., waiting in vain. At that point, I had to be honest with myself. I love my work, but I cannot allow myself to be disrespected this way. If I were being well paid, maybe I could overlook some of these frustrations. But with no money, no consistent work, and no respect, I had reached my limit.

I decided then and there to walk away. Enough was enough.

Frustrated about what happened with her, I decided to go out again and search for another job. I went back to all the places where I had previously applied, but none accepted my request. One by one, they all rejected me. I still remember going to a coffee shop where the main manager had told me the week before to come back and meet him.

He approached me with a polite smile and said, "Hello."

I replied, "Hello."

He added, "Let's go to the other side."

I nodded and said, "No problem. I'm here as you asked me to come last week."

He paused for a moment, then replied, "I'm so sorry, I just hired somebody, and there is no more place available for you. But we will keep you on file."

I felt my face flush with anger. "I was here multiple times, and you asked me to come back today. Now you're telling me you hired someone else?" Disappointed, I forced a smile and replied, "It's all good. Have a nice day," and I walked away.

I was angry, furious even, after all the effort I had put in. I decided to try another store where I had also applied. As soon as I entered, I asked politely, "Hi, please, might I speak to the manager?"

The employee at the counter looked at me and asked, "What is it for?"

"I applied for a job here a couple of weeks ago and just wanted to check on my application," I explained.

She nodded. "Ah, okay. Give me a second, I'm going to call him."

I watched them talking through the glass door. Then she returned to me and said, "Well, he said he's very busy right now and is not accepting any applications at this time."

Furious again, I left. It was unbelievable he couldn't even spare one minute to come out to the lobby and speak to me directly. Instead, he sent an employee to dismiss me. Wonderful. I hope none of you ever experience this kind of rejection because it feels like swallowing bitter medicine. We are constantly being rejected, discriminated against for no clear reason, and there is no one to complain to. You simply have to digest it in silence. The sting of rejection cuts so deep that it plants a bitterness in you, to the point that you start disliking certain people for no reason.

Still, I kept going. I didn't want to give up. I bought a train ticket and went downtown, hoping to find something. But nothing came of it. The way managers looked at me, dismissing me with the same rehearsed words, "Sorry, we are not hiring at the moment," while a bold *Hiring* sign stood at the front door, was unbelievable.

At one restaurant, I tried to approach the manager about a job. "Hi, I'm interested in joining your team," I said.

He looked me in the eyes and replied, "Oh sorry, we are not hiring at the moment."

I pointed toward the door. "But the hiring sign is right there."

He shrugged casually. "Oh, sorry! I forgot to take the sign down."

I stared at him for a second, then walked out. They made it clear: only certain people were welcome to work with them. Forcing yourself into a place where you aren't wanted will only make life miserable.

Life is already hard so hard that I sometimes don't understand why people make it worse with their poor choices and discriminatory behavior. Giving someone a chance at a job, giving them a way to survive, should be considered a blessing, not a burden. Those who have never gone days without eating, or never walked around with empty pockets, can't understand this struggle. But those of us who have endured it even once know better. Humanity seems to be reserved for a select few. Where is the humanitarian spirit? Or does it only apply when it concerns certain groups? What a shame.

We live in a society where everyone seems kind and friendly on social media, where people pose as life coaches, inviting others to do good and spread positivity. But behind the screen, in real life, they act in ways that contradict everything they preach. Poor society indeed.

A week later, my work as a personal assistant still wasn't working out. Finally, I decided to end my contract. My boss and I had been scheduled to meet on Tuesday. She never notified me of a cancellation until I texted her. That's when she said she wasn't going to the location with me anymore. Instead, she suggested Thursday. I waited for confirmation, but she never responded. Then Thursday morning arrived, and she messaged me again, saying she was too busy to meet. She asked if I was available Saturday morning instead: "Good morning, Poupy, I can't go downtown today because I have an all-day filming shoot. Are you free Saturday late morning?"

I replied firmly: "Sorry, Jacky, I'm no longer available to work as your personal assistant. I can't commit to this when I'm not even doing 10 or 20 hours per week. Please find someone else. I highly appreciate that you chose me, but unfortunately this is not working for me."

A couple of hours later, she texted again: "Hi Poupy, can we chat on the phone tomorrow, please?"

I ignored her message. I had had enough. People need to respect others just as they expect to be respected. Just because you are paying someone does not mean you have the right to treat them poorly. I agreed to work with her in good faith, but she constantly canceled meetings, barely communicated, and once even read my email report three weeks late. That is not professional. I was done. To anyone reading this, my advice is simple: know your worth, and never accept disrespect.

Back to job searching. It was one of the toughest periods of my life, and you have no idea how exhausting it was. Three months had already passed since I left my previous job because of discrimination and mistreatment, and still, I hadn't found a new one.

Today is Saturday, a beautiful sunny day. While most people are getting ready to dress up for the beach, restaurants, or a relaxing walk, I am out sweating, walking from one place to another, desperately searching for a job. Things have become so difficult that even server jobs are out of reach. At one restaurant, I humbly asked if they had a dishwasher position available. They said no that role had already been taken. I laughed bitterly, but inside I was crying. Imagine, even with a degree, I couldn't secure a simple dishwasher job. Wonderful.

That day, I printed at least ten copies of my résumé and went from store to store, restaurant to restaurant, handing them out, hoping at least one would call me back. I was struggling so badly that I reached out to my mom for help. She was confused.

"Didn't you say you were working as a personal assistant?" she asked.

Ashamed, I replied, "Yes, but not anymore. She wasn't scheduling me enough, and therefore wasn't paying me properly."

I felt terrible. We had just lost our father, and here I was asking my mother for money instead of supporting her. What a shame. But I told myself I'd rather ask her for help than go to the streets for a few dollars or do something dishonorable for survival.

I pride myself on being disciplined and respectful. I don't want to compromise my values just to get by. I believe in God's process and in the promise of a brighter future. Life is hard, yes, but don't make it worse by doing things you'll regret later. Do what makes you proud, not what fills you with shame. Because what happens in the dark always comes to light.

Eight months later, in July, the case was finally sent to the district attorney for evaluation. Yet no decision had been announced as to whether Ted would be charged. To this day, he has never been arrested or even properly interrogated by law enforcement, though I still believe that time will come. This is the last step, the final process, and I hold on to that hope.

This entire situation with Ted left scars deeper than I can fully explain. It made me dislike not only my career but my life itself. I never imagined falling in love with someone like him, yet I truly did. And I cannot deny that I loved him with a kind of passion I had never felt before. When the police officer asked me, "Is there another reason you didn't come to us right after the incident happened?" I told the truth: "I was scared, ashamed." But the hidden reason was love. I was in love with him and didn't want to denounce him. I wanted to protect the relationship, to fight for a love I thought was worth saving. But I was wrong, and the officer probably saw it in my eyes.

Today, I've decided to close the door on that chapter and give up everything I had accomplished until now in journalism. I've chosen to return to school and study Diplomacy and International Relations. Diving into something new will keep me alive, joyful, and purposeful especially because I have always loved discussions about international conflicts, immigration, and peace. I'm closing the journalism career I built with sweat and sacrifice. Maybe one day I will return as an international expert, but for now, I know this is the right path. My dream is to become a diplomat, to travel the world, to help resolve crises, and most importantly, to teach women to love and value themselves no matter what they go through.

People often ask me, "But what about kids?" I usually reply, half frustrated and half joking: "Do you think you have kids by drinking water? Or by eating a hamburger?" No, it doesn't work that way. You need a partner who also desires children. Without that, you risk ending up as a single mother, which I don't want. I love children, and children love me too. But I've never had the opportunity to meet all my nephews back home, and I miss them deeply. If I get the chance, I'll seize it in an instant.

The school I applied to is in New York, and if accepted, I'll be moving there by the end of this year to begin my new career in 2025. I'm proud of myself because I did what I came here to do in Los Angeles. I attended college, graduated, worked in newspapers and magazines, covered red carpets things I knew would have been impossible for a Black African woman back home. I laughed, I cried, I was rejected, humiliated, intimidated, but those very experiences shaped me. They are what make my story fascinating.

I knew from the start that I didn't have the skin color or the look most people want to see on TV. But I still wanted to challenge myself, to prove to myself that I could do it. With everything going on in Africa, we need more journalists from our own communities telling our own stories, not outsiders repeating the same narratives. That was my motivation.

I remember when my sister and my mother called me one day, urging me to leave journalism and return to nursing. They told me bluntly: "You are not white, and you are not mixed. How could you possibly think you can get a good job there?" Their words hurt deeply, but they were also true. I didn't want to see it, but I knew. I was broke, struggling to survive, even though I was passionate about journalism. I had invested years of education and energy, yet the financial return was almost nothing. I had even reached the point of relying on my mother to support me. That was painful and unacceptable. But I don't regret trying. At least I can say I gave my best.

I never compare my life with others. There are people who were born here, who had every opportunity, yet never accomplished half of what I did since arriving. I know for my family, their biggest concern has always been marriage and children. But how am I supposed to marry and have children if I don't even have a serious boyfriend? I know the time will come. One day I'll meet the man meant for me the prince I dream of, with whom I'll have two children, a boy and a girl. Then, all this suffering will become nothing more than memory.

I've reached out to friends some close, others more distant but none of them truly helped me. Some ignored my calls and messages. Others told me bluntly to quit journalism and become a CNA in a nursing home. It's in moments like this you learn who your real friends are, and who never were. Even my aunt, who had once accepted money from me when I was supporting her, told me to come back home since I was struggling here. "There's a place for you here," she said. I laughed bitterly. Yes, maybe someday I'll return home, but not now. I still have so much to achieve, so much to prove to myself.

Then, as if God had been quietly listening to my cries, I received a notification from the California Victim Compensation Board regarding my abuse case. When I saw it, I felt joy rush through me. I wanted to cry tears of relief, but for once, I didn't. I kept it to myself. I didn't tell friends or family because I've learned over time: not everyone deserves to know your victories.

Like someone once said, "Use your pain to reinvent yourself." That is exactly what I did. This unexpected financial breakthrough reminded me that patience and resilience eventually pay off. You must rise, fight, and believe in yourself even when the world tries to break you. Accept people's criticism if you must, write down the

94

lessons, but never let others define your destiny. At the end of the day, only you know what is best for yourself. Not your friends. Not your family. Not anyone.

For real, Los Angeles is very expensive, and life here is incredibly tough. With inflation, things have only become worse. People often feel fake, shallow, sometimes even mindless. They will smile at you in your face and then turn around to trash you behind your back, discarding you like used toilet paper. That is the sad reality of the city a place where appearances dominate and sincerity is rare.

But in the middle of that, I consider myself lucky. My landlord is a Korean man named James. He is very friendly, approachable, and, like me, an immigrant who came here determined to make it in Hollywood. He chose to invest in real estate, and today he is doing really well for himself. Unlike many others, James has empathy. When I shared my story with him, he didn't dismiss me or judge me he listened. That small act of humanity meant everything to me.

One day, I even decided to donate everything I had won during a TV game show back to this place, as a way to show my gratitude for his kindness. Since then, I was blessed to receive three months of free rent, which came directly from the value of the prize I had won. It felt like God was rewarding me for doing the right thing. Sometimes in life, you have to learn to do good for others not because you expect something back, but because goodness has a way of finding its way back to you. And when it comes, it is often multiplied.

Had I been living somewhere else, I probably would have already been kicked out by now. But here, I see the power of grace and kindness. God is good. Thank you, Lord.

Chapter 8: Court and End

After careful evaluation, The District Attorney's office has finally reached a decision on the case against Ted. I was told to come to the courthouse to hear it in person. Will there be any media coverage? What is going to happen? Don't miss any part of this chapter.

The big day was finally here. It was a sunny Wednesday morning. The meeting was set at 8:30 at the superior court. I woke up early, felt a little stressed but also confident. I ate breakfast and drank a cup of tea. Then I got ready for the big day. I put on a blue navy jacket and black skirt to look professional and classy at the same time. I ordered an Uber to the location and was there 45 minutes early. My lawyer and his team joined me and they made a kind gesture and assured me to remain calm and relaxed.

A few minutes later, the defendant's party came. Ted's eyes and mine crossed and the atmosphere was salty. I kept my confidence and decided not to be intimidated by him or his team. 8:30 a.m. clicked and a court officer opened the door. Gave everybody instructions. Turn phones off or put them on silence. Have a seat inside. Indicate if anyone needs a translator or not.

Once inside, a court official came out and took a seat. She opened her laptop and turned on the screen in front of her. She saluted the audience and gave some additional instructions too, then proceeded to check the list for the day. After everything was confirmed, the assistant asked everyone to wait before the District Attorney's representative made their appearance.

When the representative entered, the room fell silent. He carried a solemn demeanor and requested to speak to both legal teams privately for a moment. The wait was agonizing. After what felt like an eternity, my lawyer returned to my side. His face was grim. He explained that the District Attorney had reviewed the case one final time and, with a heavy heart, he informed me that the case was being formally dismissed due to insufficient evidence to proceed to trial. The state would not be pressing charges.

The air left my lungs. It wasn't that we had lost; the fight itself had been called off. The rest of the day was difficult. A lot of prayers, no sleep, no appetite.

The next day, Thursday morning, I met with my team to process the outcome. We gathered in a quiet room in the same courthouse, the absence of a crowd feeling louder than any verdict. The reality was a very cold atmosphere. The system had found that the evidence, my truth, was insufficient. There would be no handcuffs, no sentencing, no judgment to pay.

It was a devastating moment for me and my team. After a long time of fighting, the path to legal justice had closed. Outside the courthouse, a few media outlets were waiting. With my head held high, I told them that while the state wouldn't be proceeding, it didn't change the truth. I mentioned that for a long time black women have been abused and discriminated against, often without legal recourse or validation, but that our voices matter. This was not the end, but a painful step in the long journey for Black Immigrants' rights.

I addressed my gratitude to my whole team, my lawyers especially, because they believed in me when the system stopped. To my professor who motivated me to go to the police and report him, which was not easy for me. To my two therapists who, despite their busy schedules, found a moment to speak and meet with me. To all my family members for their kind text messages and prayers and to my friends who checked on me often. Big thank you to all of you; this journey and my strength wouldn't have happened without you.

Love you all.!!!!!!!

The law is not always just. But we must never stop seeking what is right.

Question: Was I wrong to fall in love with him? Or did I just meet the wrong person? I'm still looking for the right answer.

Author's Note

After writing this book, I came to a painful but liberating conclusion: I was dealing with a narcissist, a manipulator, without realizing it. Just because someone is handsome or kind in appearance does not mean he is not dangerous. He made me doubt myself, blame myself, and question my own reactions to his rudeness and disrespect. I was blinded by love, but in reality, there was no love on his part only control, only manipulation. I began to notice patterns: no empathy when my father passed away, no support when I lost my job, no encouragement as I struggled to grow my business. Meanwhile, I was making every effort to see him, to meet his needs, to be there, despite my own busy schedule and challenges. And let me be clear: I never asked him to pay my bills. I paid for my tuition myself until graduation. I built my business with my own effort. After four months of this so-called relationship with no growth, no positive change in my life I finally began to question its very nature. He refused to change, so I chose to leave. He didn't appreciate it, but I had to. Because I love myself. And loving myself means giving myself the treatment I deserve.

To anyone reading this: do not stay with a narcissist. Do not make excuses. It is not healthy mentally, emotionally, or physically. It will drain you until you lose yourself, until the joy of life disappears. Even therapy can feel powerless against the depth of pain they cause. I was diagnosed with PTSD by my therapist. For months, I locked myself inside my room, isolating myself from the world. For six to eight months, I lived in silence, alone with my scars. No medicine could fix it only time, resilience, and faith. Two years have passed. I have chosen to move forward. Life still brings obstacles, some that I cannot explain. For example, in December 2024, I finally secured a new office job at the airport, scheduled to start on January 15, 2025. I felt excited a chance to rebuild, to meet new people, to embrace a new environment. But life intervened again. A wildfire struck the city, raging for a week, destroying homes, businesses, cars. The training was postponed. Then ICE raids swept through, arresting immigrants, spreading fear and anxiety everywhere. It felt like one setback after another.

But today, after many attempts, after so much rejection, I finally received a call from Robert, the hiring manager. He told me to start tomorrow. And with that, a new chapter begins.

This book, *Get Up and Fight*, is more than my story. It is a testament that no matter where you come from, if you are determined and ambitious, you can still find your place in the world. You will face discrimination, rejection, abuse, and countless forms of injustice but if you believe, if you stand strong, you can fight for your rights and claim the justice you deserve. Domestic violence is real. It destroys lives. It nearly destroyed mine. I used to believe it could never happen to me until it did. If you are a victim, know this: there may be no words that fully capture your pain, but you are not alone. Be brave. Reach out. Call emergency services if you are in danger. File a police report. Protect yourself. And to the abusers: you may think that your money, your power, your influence can shield you. You may believe your victim's cries cannot touch you. You are wrong. You may win today, but tomorrow justice will stand in front of you stronger than you ever imagined. Change is possible, but only if you choose to. Seek help. Take classes. Break the cycle before it consumes you too.

To my readers: thank you for walking with me through this journey. I share my story not just for myself, but for every woman, every immigrant, every survivor who feels voiceless. Remember: no one is above the law. And more importantly no one has the right to take away your dignity, your peace, or your hope.

Love yourself enough to fight. And when you fall, *get up and fight again.*

Building a Legacy, One Victory at a Time

About the Author

My name is Poupy Gaelle Kenfack Nguetsop, born in Douala, Cameroon, Central Africa. I am the eldest of five siblings, single, and without children. Growing up, I watched my parents work tirelessly to give us a better life. My father, an entrepreneur and founder of GPM Group, was decorated three times for his achievements and remained my greatest role model until his passing. My mother, once an insurance salesperson, became my inspiration for kindness, discipline, and perseverance.

I earned my Bachelor's degree in Nursing in 2014 and worked in healthcare and insurance before moving to the United States. In June 2023, I graduated from Los Angeles City College with a degree in Journalism. Alongside my studies, I pursued media, modeling, and acting, appearing in shows such as *Lethal Weapon, Snowfall, How to Get Away With Murder, House of Cards, S.W.A.T.*, and more. I also modeled for campaigns, including one that featured on a Los Angeles City College billboard for a year, and appeared on TV game shows like *Let's Make a Deal* and *Judge Judy Show*.

For four years, I covered Hollywood red-carpet events, including the Hollywood Christmas Parade, HollyShorts Film Festival, and the Los Angeles International Film Festival. In 2023, I was honored as a California Humanities Project Fellowship recipient, and in 2024, I volunteered for Robert F. Kennedy Jr.'s presidential campaign, where interviewing him marked a defining moment in my career.

Beyond my achievements, I am an advocate for immigrants, especially African immigrants, who face discrimination and rejection. My mission is to fight for equality, dignity, and representation for all.

www.ingramcontent.com/pod-product-compliance
Lightning Source LLC
Chambersburg PA
CBHW071532120626
46550CB00006B/2430